ABRAHAM KUYPER

ABRAHAM KUYPER

A Short and Personal Introduction

Richard J. Mouw

William B. Eerdmans Publishing Company

Grand Rapids, Michigan / Cambridge, U.K.

Published 2011 by

Wm. B. Eerdmans Publishing Co.

2140 Oak Industrial Drive N.E., Grand Rapids, Michigan 49505 /

P.O. Box 163, Cambridge CB3 9PU U.K.

Printed in the United States of America

21 20 19 18 17 16   9 8 7 6 5 4

2018-09

Library of Congress Cataloging-in-Publication Data

Mouw, Richard J.

Abraham Kuyper : a short and personal introduction / Richard J. Mouw.

p.   cm.

ISBN 978-0-8028-6603-5 (pbk. : alk. paper)

1. Kuyper, Abraham, 1837–1920.   I. Title.

BX9479.K8M68   2011

284′.2092 — dc22

[B]

2011004909

www.eerdmans.com

Contents

———⊸⊶⊷⊶⊷⊶⊷⊸———

[v]

Contents

Introduction

———⌘———

T his book about Abraham Kuyper is both short and personal.

I decided to make it *short* because I want to introduce some basics about Kuyper's thought for readers who may be curious enough about this nineteenth-century Dutch leader to read a fairly concise introduction. Kuyper has some enthusiastic devotees in the English-speaking world, and there are probably some out there who wonder what all the fuss is about, even though they may not be eager to know every detail. This book is meant to satisfy that kind of curiosity. There is a growing body of excellent and detailed scholarly commentary on Kuyper's views on many subjects, but my intention here is to offer something that will be read by folks who might not make their way through some of those other writings — or, better yet, who may need a nudge in the direction of more serious engagement.

But this is also a very *personal* introduction to Kuyper. Abraham Kuyper covered a lot of subjects, and I am not even going to begin to cover all of the ground he covered. My focus is going to be on the Kuyper who lured me in.

Introduction

The Lure of Kuyper

I encountered Kuyper as a formative influence during the last half of the 1960s. It wasn't that he had been a total stranger prior to that period in my life; I had actually read one of his long theological treatises, *Principles of Sacred Theology,* when it was an assigned textbook in a seminary course that I had taken earlier in the decade. Yet only when I turned to Kuyper's writings about issues of public life did I find exactly what I urgently needed.

In the late 1960s I found myself immersed in the turmoil of secular university campus life. It precipitated a crisis of faith for me, as I wrestled much with how I as a Christian should be dealing with some of the big issues being debated in American public life. This was the time of the civil rights movement and the bitter debates about the legitimacy of the war in Vietnam.

I felt ill-prepared for these challenges as an evangelical Christian. I had been raised in the kind of evangelical environment where the life of the mind was not held in high regard. We were suspicious of "worldly learning." I had made my way out of that kind of anti-intellectualism, but I still was not sure where to look for help in finding an alternative to the "other-worldly" mentality of my younger years. I had been told often that getting involved in "social action" was not the kind of thing God wanted from us. One of the favorite lines I heard from preachers as a kid was that trying to improve things here on earth is like trying to rearrange the deck chairs on the Titanic. The attitude we were to have toward "this world" was summed up nicely in a song we often sang:

This world is not my home, I'm just a-passing through.
My treasures are laid up somewhere beyond the blue.

Introduction

The angels beckon me from heaven's open door,
and I can't feel at home in this world anymore.

Eager to distance myself from that mentality — especially given the pressures of the activist sixties — I explored other theological alternatives. But it was a frustrating time for me spiritually and theologically. I was not attracted to a liberal "social gospel" approach. And while the social teachings of the Catholic tradition made some sense to me, I was not ready to travel the road to Rome.

It was during this time that I came upon Abraham Kuyper's *Lectures on Calvinism,* the Stone Lectures that he had delivered at Princeton Seminary during his 1898 visit to the United States. In Kuyper's robust Calvinism I discovered what I had been looking for: a vision of active involvement in public life that would allow me to steer my way between a privatized evangelicalism on the one hand and the liberal Protestant or Catholic approaches to public discipleship on the other hand. I have attempted to walk in this way ever since.

Focusing on Culture

Because what I will be discussing in these pages is my own personal "take" on Kuyper, I will purposely be concentrating on what I am calling his theology of culture. To be sure, there is a lot more to Kuyper. He addressed many audiences and in many formats. He authored technical works on difficult theological topics; he gave speeches to farmers' associations and labor unions; he preached sermons and wrote meditations on biblical texts; and as a highly visible politician he articulated positions on countless matters of public policy. So I am going to be very selective in what I cover here.

To say all of that, of course, is itself an important introduction to Kuyper. If someone were to make a list of the most energetic "multitaskers" in the history of Christian thought, Abraham Kuyper would certainly rank high. He founded a newspaper, a university, a political party, and a denomination. Nor was he content to start something and then move on to a different project. During his career, which lasted from his ordination in the 1860s until his death in 1920, he regularly wrote articles for his newspaper; he taught theology at the Free University; he led his party both as a member of the Dutch parliament and, for a few years, as Prime Minister. And all the while he played an active role in the life (and controversies) of the Dutch Reformed churches, often addressing the issues by writing major theological books and essays.

The influence of Kuyper's thought has long been felt in the Reformed — especially Dutch Calvinist — branch of American evangelicalism, but more recently the interest in his ideas has extended beyond those circles. His name turns up these days in more general discussions of Christian social thought and civil society, and his views are often compared to, or contrasted with, the Puritan political traditions, the liberal "social gospel" theology, recent Catholic social thought, and contemporary explorations in the social sciences.

The North American interest in Kuyper has now been advanced significantly by the establishing in 2002 of the Abraham Kuyper Center for Public Theology at Princeton Theological Seminary. The Center, which houses a major collection of Kuyper-related materials, sponsors an annual Kuyper Prize Lecture, accompanied by a conference on Kuyperian topics, as well as publishing the *The Kuyper Center Review*.

Introduction

An Important Voice

I have written this short and personal introduction to Kuyper because I am convinced his voice continues to speak in important ways. He certainly can be a big help to evangelical Protestants in the United States. During one of the public debates over potential justices for the United States Supreme Court, a political journalist observed that evangelical Protestants regularly make a lot of noise about such matters, but when conservative candidates come to the fore, they are typically Roman Catholics. The pundit remarked that this was a sign that evangelical Protestantism, in contrast to Catholicism, lacks "intellectual heft."[1]

That journalist had it pretty much right when it comes to theological perspectives on questions of public policy. Evangelicals have been a prominent presence in public life in recent years, but we have not been known for having a coherent theological-philosophical perspective on our efforts to influence the policies and practices of the larger society. Kuyper can be an important guide in this regard. As we will see, there is plenty in Kuyper that needs updating and even serious correcting. Yet almost a century after his passing, he still has some vital insights to offer about Christian cultural and political discipleship.

1. Franklin Foer, "How Catholics Became the Brain Behind Evangelical Politics," http://hnn.us/roundup/entries/17993.html.

Kuyper on Theology and Culture:
An Overview

Kuyper's Calvinism

⚬⚬⚬

Kuyper started off his career as a Dutch Reformed pastor who was deeply influenced by the liberal theology that he had been taught at the University of Leiden. But in the rural village where he served his first pastorate he encountered parishioners who exhibited a vibrant evangelical faith, and through his contacts with them he experienced a life-changing evangelical conversion. The person who initially influenced him in this regard was Pietje Baltus, the young daughter of a miller. Pietje was known in the community to be a person of deep spirituality, but she did not regularly attend the worship services, choosing instead to meet in private homes with others who shared her Calvinist faith.

When Kuyper found out that she was boycotting his services because of the content of his preaching, he paid her a pastoral visit. When he arrived at her home, she refused to shake his hand. This was a gesture of disrespect, and she was obviously signaling her rejection of his pastoral authority. Instead of being offended, though, Kuyper listened carefully to what she had to say, and he made a point of pursuing further conversations with Pietje and her friends. Later he wrote: "I did not set myself against them, and I still thank my God that I made the choice I did. Their unwavering persistence has been a blessing for my heart, the rise of the morning star in my life."[1]

Creation's "Square Inches"

Having embraced evangelical Calvinism, Kuyper ever thereafter placed a strong emphasis on personal piety. In the midst of his busy public career he wrote hundreds of meditations about the need for the individual believer to turn away from the demands of the active life and retreat into that very private sacred space where the soul is alone with her Maker.

But Kuyper was not content with a religion that was limited to the cultivation of a purely personal spirituality. In addition to his celebration of the experience of a Savior's love, he also placed a strong emphasis on the supreme Lordship of Jesus Christ over all spheres of social, political, and economic life. Kuyper's followers are fond of quoting the manifesto he issued at Free University's inaugural convocation: "There is not a square inch in the whole domain of our human existence over which Christ, who is sovereign over all, does not cry 'Mine!'"[2]

That manifesto is a good summary of his overall perspective. Calvinism is well known for its insistence that we are

1. Quoted in Louis Praamsma, *Let Christ Be King: Reflections on the Life and Times of Abraham Kuyper* (Jordan Station, Ont.: Paideia Press, 1985), 49.

2. Abraham Kuyper, "Sphere Sovereignty," in *Abraham Kuyper: A Centennial Reader,* ed. James D. Bratt (Grand Rapids: Eerdmans, 1998), 488.

saved by grace alone, and that God "elects" those who are to be recipients of this saving grace. This perspective focuses on human sinfulness and divine sovereignty. Out of sheer mercy God does for human beings what they cannot do for themselves. He reaches into the depths of a human heart and irresistibly draws that person to himself.

Many think that's all they need to know about Calvinism. But Kuyper was not content to leave it there. When God saves us, he insisted, he incorporates us into a community, the people of God. And this community, in turn, is called to serve God's goals in the larger world. In the life of the church we worship a sovereign God, but that God then commands us to be active witnesses in our daily lives to God's sovereign rule over all things.

For Kuyper, every Christian is called to be an agent of the Kingdom of Jesus Christ, wherever they are called by God to serve. The system of thought that Kuyper developed was an elaborate spelling out of how we are to understand this call to Kingdom service. How are we to understand God's intentions in creating the world and — in response to the human rebellion that thwarted God's creating purposes — in sending the divine Son to reclaim the world that had been so corrupted by sin? Given the continuing presence of sin in the world, how are Christians best to structure and pursue their Kingdom service "out there" in the near and far reaches of the creation? These are the questions that motivated much of Kuyper's thinking about how Christians are to serve the Lord in the broad reaches of culture.

"Filling the Earth"

—— ⚬⚬⚬ ——

I ntroductions to the study of culture often begin by observing that "culture" carries the meaning of "cultivation." Thus, agriculture is the cultivation of the *agros,* Greek for "field"; horticulture is the cultivation of plants; and so on. When we use the word "culture" to apply to human realities, we are referring to the ways in which we human beings cultivate patterns and processes that give meaning to our collective interactions, as well as the things that we "grow" as a result of those interactions.

The Cultural Mandate

For Kuyper, God cares deeply about culture and its development — *so* deeply that the divine desire that human beings engage in cultural activity was a central motive for God's creating the world. In the narrative of Genesis 1, immediately after creating human beings in God's own image, God gives them instructions about how to behave in the garden.

In the three-part mandate of Genesis 1:28, the first thing God tells them is to "be fruitful and multiply." That is about reproduction. He wants them to procreate, to have children. But when the Lord immediately goes on to tell them to "fill the earth," that is a different assignment. This "filling" mandate, as viewed by Kuyper and others in the Reformed tradition, is a call to cultural activity — "the cultural mandate." The first humans are placed in a garden — the raw nature of plants, animals, soil, and rocks — and they are instructed to introduce something new into that garden: the processes and products of human culture.

When the Creator goes on to stipulate that they are to "have dominion" over the garden, that means they must manage — rule over — these patterns and processes of culture in obedience to God's will. In the well-known formulation of the Westminster Shorter Catechism, our "chief end" as created human beings "is to glorify God and to enjoy him forever" — and at the heart of this glorifying our Maker is our obedient service as God's designated caretakers in the cultural aspects of created life. Our true "enjoyment" includes our flourishing in the kind of participation in created life that God intends for us.

Here is a simple way of illustrating how all that cultural "filling" activity was meant to go. Imagine a scenario of this sort for the first pair of humans. On their first day together, Adam and Eve decide that they should clear away one small area of the garden as their domestic space, and Adam begins brushing away leaves and twigs with his hands. "No, no! Try this," Eve says to him, and she breaks a large branch off a nearby tree and strips it of some of its smaller branches. She then uses it to brush leaves and twigs away, in order to create a clear space on the ground. "See," she says, "we can use this.

[7]

Let's call it a *rake*. And I'll be the one who uses it today and then after that we'll take turns every other day clearing away the leaves and twigs."

In that brief transaction, several projects of cultural formation have already taken place. They have begun to "fill the earth." Eve has created a piece of *technology:* out of raw nature she has fashioned a tool. She has transformed a mere stick into a cultural artifact. Then she has given it a name — "rake" — thus articulating a rudimentary *labeling system*. She has also outlined a pattern of social organization for *distributing labor* — "we'll take turns" — as well as setting up a *schedule*. In all of this she has added several things to the primary garden environment that the Creator has designed, thus developing a new level of human-fashioned reality that is being superimposed upon the raw nature of the garden.

Human Rebellion

That was what God intended for the unfallen creation: that human beings would "fill the earth" by working with the stuff of nature to produce culture. Unfortunately, though, things did not go smoothly. Human beings rebelled against God and disrupted the original design for the creation and for their role in it. What is important for Kuyper's account, though, is that the fact of our fallenness does not in any way diminish either the reality or the importance of cultural formation. What human rebellion against the will of God does introduce into the picture is that now we have two very different patterns of cultural formation in the world: cultural disobedience as well as cultural obedience.

The Fall occurred when human beings gave into the temptation presented to them by the Serpent. God has told them not to eat the fruit from one of the trees in the garden, and the Serpent challenges them to go ahead and eat it anyway. God is not to be trusted. God knows, says the Serpent, that "when you eat of it your eyes will be opened, and you will be like God" (Genesis 3:5).

This understanding of the nature of sin is crucial for grasping Kuyper's overall system of thought. He is following the traditional theological idea — featured prominently in the thinking of theologians like St. Augustine and John Calvin — that sin is essentially a state of "ethical rebellion." Sin does not consist simply in the awareness of our finitude, or a basic anxiety that emerges out of that awareness. The Fall was not about finitude as such, since human beings were at one time both finite and unfallen. What introduced sin into the created order was an act of will, a rebellion against the command of God.

Rejecting the Enlightenment

There is an element in Kuyper's thinking on this subject that has an interesting link to the way present-day "postmodern" thinkers discuss the defects of "the Enlightenment project." Enlightenment thought saw human reason — or more generally, an enlightened human consciousness — as the highest standard in the universe for deciding issues of truth and goodness. On that view, if there is anything worthwhile in religion, it conforms to or even reinforces what we "enlightened" human beings can come to know without the aid of any sort of revelation.

The postmodern thinkers who are asking us to reject that

Enlightenment way of viewing things are not, of course, asking us to turn to God as the source of meaning and truth. Instead, they are insisting that we human beings are incapable of rising above our finitude; there is no "meta-narrative" — no above-it-all way of viewing things that allows us to critique our individual "social locations" from a perspective informed by "universal reason."

Like the postmodern thinkers, Kuyper rejected the notion that an enlightened human consciousness can give us access to reliable answers to the big issues of life. Of course, he would disagree with them when they make the creative human will the supreme standard. It is God's will that governs all things; our own wills need to be turned away from our sinful projects and brought into harmony with the divine will.

Corrupted Culture

When Eve and Adam succumbed to the Serpent's challenge, then, they turned their wills away from God and placed their ultimate trust in something less than God. This had ramifications for their relationship not only with their Maker, but also with each other and with the rest of creation. They looked at each other in new ways, with suspicion and a propensity for conflict. And the larger creation now fell under a general curse.

To put it mildly, all of this has had very serious effects on cultural activity. Prior to the Fall, the processes and products of culture were directed toward glorifying God; the human pair were managing their cultural activity in obedience to God. After the Fall, the cultural mandate of "filling the earth" underwent a serious change.

Sin certainly does not put an end to cultural activity, but it does pervert it. Not long after the story of Adam and Eve being expelled from Eden, we learn that numbered among their immediate descendents was Jabal, "the ancestor of those who live in tents and have livestock"; Jubal, "the ancestor of all those who play the lyre and pipe"; and Tubal-cain, a craftsman, "who made all kinds of bronze and iron tools" (Genesis 4:20-22). But now all of this cultural activity is scarred by sinful rebellion. While technology, for example, was originally meant to facilitate service to God as a means of managing and enjoying the created order, soon rebellious humans defiantly attempted to "build ourselves a city, and a tower with its top in the heavens," so as "to make a name for ourselves" (Genesis 11:4).

These distortions of cultural activity brought about by sin, however, have not irreparably damaged the good creation. The situation is not one of a total obliteration of God's original designs. Kuyper would enthusiastically endorse what H. Richard Niebuhr said about the "transforming culture" theme in his classic *Christ and Culture* book. Culture, says Niebuhr, has been become distorted and perverted because of human sin. But the corruption that we see, he also insists, "is all corrupted order rather than order *for* corruption. . . . It is perverted good, not evil; or it is evil as perversion and not as badness of being."[1]

A New Initiative

Human rebellion made a mess of what God originally intended for the creation. But those angry rebellious cries —

---

1. H. Richard Niebuhr, *Christ and Culture* (San Francisco: Harper and Row, 1951), 194, emphasis added.

echoing the "we will be our own gods" of Genesis 3 — were not the final words about the human condition. God looked down upon this rebellious humanity and decided to start something new. He decided to choose a specific people — the ethnic Israelites, Abraham's descendents — to be special recipients of his sovereign grace. He called them to organize their lives so as to show the rest of the world what it is like to live in obedience to the will of the Creator in all dimensions of human life. He gave them instructions not only about how to worship, but also about farming, family life, politics, economics, the fashioning of beautiful things, their relationships with other tribes and nations — in short, God chose Israel as a means of putting on display some of his original intentions for cultural processes and products. Once again there would be people on the earth who would direct their lives toward his glory, "filling the earth" and "having dominion" in ways that pleased the Creator.

The initiative that God took with ancient Israel, however, was the first stage of something much more significant that God would eventually bring about. There came a time when the eternal God appeared in the flesh, as Jesus of Nazareth, to guarantee the success of the initiative begun in more ancient times. It is important to note that the most widely quoted New Testament verse about the coming of Christ, John 3:16, isn't just about God's desire to save individual souls. It certainly *includes* that, but there is more. The Greek word translated as "world" is *cosmos,* which is properly understood as referring to the original created order: "For God so loved the *cosmos* that he gave his only Son, so that everyone who believes in him may not perish but may have eternal life." And this is immediately followed by a wonderful piece of assurance in verse 17: that "God did not send the Son into the *cosmos* to condemn the *cosmos*, but in order that the *cosmos* might be saved through him."

This points us to a much bigger Christ than is often understood by evangelicals, the same cosmic Christ that the Apostle Paul describes as the One in whom "all things in heaven and on earth were created, things visible and invisible, whether thrones or dominions or rulers or powers — all things have been created through him and for him. He himself is before all things, and in him all things hold together" (Colossians 1:16-17).

Restoring Creation

Redemption is restoration. Al Wolters wrote a fine book setting forth the "Reformational worldview" inspired by Kuyper, and he gave it the title *Creation Regained.*[2] You can't really understand Kuyper's way of viewing things without grasping what that title is meant to communicate.

That the redemption accomplished by Christ heals what was wounded by the Fall is certainly true in the redeeming of individuals. When Christ redeems us he means to restore us to what God originally created human beings to be. And that emphasis on the salvation of individuals is of great importance for Kuyper. He knew in his own life what it was to experience the transforming power of the gospel of Jesus Christ. Jesus was for him a personal Savior — the One who went to the cross to rescue us from the curse of our fallen nature.

But redemption also reaches far beyond individuals. The

---

2. Al Wolters, *Creation Regained: Biblical Basics for a Reformational Worldview,* 2nd edition (Grand Rapids: Eerdmans, 2005).

John 3 passages I have just quoted make the link. Jesus came to redeem the creation, to cleanse it from the depravity that permeates the cosmos. And this redemptive operation is restorative in character. Once again God is working to fulfill the original purposes of his creating project.

This vision of the cosmic rescue mission of Jesus so inspired Kuyper that he liked to emphasize the fact that Jesus did not come to do something brand new, but to fix what had been broken by sin. Sometimes he seems to be exaggerating the "nothing new" dimension of what Christ died to accomplish. Here is a typical example of that tendency toward hyperbole, a passage from his Stone Lectures:

> Can we imagine that at one time God willed to rule things in a certain moral order, but that now, in Christ, He wills to rule it otherwise? As though He were not the Eternal, the Unchangeable, Who, from the very hour of creation, even unto all eternity, had willed, wills, and shall will and maintain, one and the same firm moral world-order! Verily Christ has swept away the dust with which man's sinful limitations had covered up this world-order, and has made it glitter again in its original brilliancy. . . . [T]he world-order remains just what it was from the beginning. It lays full claim, not only to the believer (as though less were required from the unbeliever), but to every human being and to all human relationships.[3]

Again, that may be a bit of an overstatement — it certainly is a bit overwrought for my theological tastes. But it does

---

3. Abraham Kuyper, *Lectures on Calvinism* (Grand Rapids: Eerdmans, 1931), 71-72.

make clear the important continuity that Kuyper wants to stress between creation and redemption. And it highlights his important message that our salvation as individuals includes the obligation to align ourselves with God's desire that his will is to be acknowledged and glorified in all areas of life. Our discipleship includes cultural obedience: "And whatever you do, in word or deed, do everything in the name of the Lord Jesus, giving thanks to God the Father through him" (Colossians 3:17).

The important question, of course, is: How are we to *do* that? How *are* we as Christians to work at redeemed cultural activity? What does this say to nurses and artists and lawyers and corporate managers? This is a subject to which Kuyper devoted much of his life's work, both as an activist and a theorist. We will look now at some of the major Kuyperian themes that he set forth to help us work at this task of cultural renewal.

Celebrating Many-ness

───── ✺ ─────

One of Kuyper's favorite terms was "pluriformity." He had a fondness for many-ness. This fondness shows up clearly in his doctrine of the church. He was dissatisfied with the long-standing "Christendom" arrangement that featured an intimate bond between church and state. And he was convinced that this too-intimate arrangement was grounded in the misguided assumption, as he put it, "that the Church of Christ on earth could express itself only in one form and as one institution."

The fact is, Kuyper insisted, that the true church "can reveal itself in many forms, in different countries; nay, even in the same country, in a multiplicity of institutions." He saw it as a major contribution of the sixteenth-century Reformation that it had "ruptured the unity of the Church," breaking "that one Church into fragments," in order to encourage "a rich variety of all manner of church formations."[1] Kuyper wanted us to see the "differences of climate and of nation, of historical

1. Kuyper, *Lectures,* 101.

past, and of disposition of mind" in a positive light — thus acknowledging a reality that "annihilates the absolute character of every visible church, and places them all side by side, as differing in degrees of purity, but always remaining in some way or other a manifestation of one holy and catholic Church of Christ in Heaven."[2]

Kuyper was well aware that these views would not sit well with many of his fellow Calvinists. He knew he was being "neo-" on this point in his Calvinism. But he was convinced that his positive assessment of churchly many-ness was a legitimate extension of developments that were set in motion by John Calvin himself. For one thing, he saw in Calvinism's evolving support for the idea of religious freedom — the advocacy of the rights of diverse churches to pursue their various patterns of life and worship — an implicit endorsement of the idea of ecclesiastical pluriformity. The history of Calvinism demonstrates, he said, an increasing appreciation in that tradition for "national differences of morals, differences of disposition and of emotions, [and] different degrees in depth of life and insight, [which] necessarily resulted in emphasizing first one, and then another side of the same truth."[3]

Created Complexity

Kuyper's fondness for pluriformity ran deep. He was convinced that God himself loves many-ness. Indeed, on his reading of the biblical account, the Creator had deliberately woven many-ness into the very fabric of creation. Kuyper even

2. Kuyper, *Lectures,* 63-64.
3. Kuyper, *Lectures,* 64.

wrote an essay on the subject to which he gave the telling title "Uniformity: The Curse of Modern Life."

Many-ness, Kuyper argued, was necessary for created life to flourish in a "fresh and vigorous" manner.[4] Referring to the Genesis creation story, Kuyper noted that the Lord willed "[t]hat all life should multiply 'after its kind.'" That the concept of "kind" in that context applied specifically to animal life did not deter Kuyper from making a more general application. "[E]very domain of nature," he says, displays an "infinite diversity, an inexhaustible profusion of variations." And this many-ness also rules the world of humanity, which "undulates and teems" with the same sort of diversity, bestowed upon our collective existence by a "generous God who from the riches of his glory distributed gifts, powers, aptitude, and talents to each according to his divine will."[5]

This many-ness continues under our present fallen condition. God's creation is still characterized by pluriformity. The problem is that we sinful human beings have a hard time handling this complexity. In our rebellion we tend to treat the many-ness of created life in one of two very different ways.

One sinful strategy is simply to affirm many-ness without seeing any overall coherence to the splendidly complex reality in which we find ourselves. That is a special temptation today, especially in those circles where "fragmentation" as such is a thing to be celebrated. One recent defender of the "postmodern" way of viewing reality has insisted that we are now living in "an antinomian moment" in which we must reject all "totalizing" accounts of the human condition. To refuse "the

4. Kuyper, "Uniformity: The Curse of Modern Life," in Bratt, *Abraham Kuyper: A Centennial Reader,* 25.

5. Kuyper, "Uniformity," 34.

tyranny of wholes," he says, is to learn to live comfortably with "an epistemological obsession with fragments."[6]

From Kuyper's perspective this misses a crucial point about the many-ness of reality, namely, the teaching set forth so clearly in the Apostle's affirmation of the supreme Lordship of Christ. The Son of God is the unifying and integrating One; "in him all things hold together" (Colossians 1:17).

This does not mean that the integration comes easily. Contemporary life is very complex. I struggle with that complexity all the time. How do I tie together all of the varied roles that are so much a part of my everyday life? I am, among other things, a husband, a father, a grandfather, a teacher, an administrator, a church member, and one who needs rest and recreation. How do I set my priorities among these many "fragments"?

It's not easy. But as a Christian I have to take these questions to the Lord. I know that he holds it all together and that by seeing all of these things in the context of his integrating Lordship, I can continually sort things out. I don't simply have to give in to a many-ness that has no ultimate coherence.

The second sinful strategy is to try to get rid of some or all of the many-ness by squeezing things together, in a way that this or that element of the many-ness begins to choke out the others. Either God is at the center of our lives or something else is. And if it is something else, then it is something that is less than the true God. This means that we will be devoted to the service of something *within* the creaturely realm, treating that created something as if it has an ultimate worth that be-

6. Iban Hassan, quoted in Richard Bernstein, *The New Constellation: The Ethical-Political Horizons of Modernity/Postmodernity* (Boston: MIT Press, 1992), 199.

longs properly to God alone. And then we tend to make that one thing the factor that unifies and organizes everything else.

When sociologist Robert Bellah and his associates were researching their 1985 book, *Habits of the Heart,* they interviewed a woman named Sheila, who, when they asked her about her basic convictions about life, told them that her religion was "Sheila-ism" — following the dictates of, she said, "just my own little voice."[7] That is about as simple as idolatry can get: make yourself the center of everything in life, doing only what your inner "Sheila" voice tells you to do.

But idolatry can take other forms, some of them significantly more subtle than Sheila-ism. The creation is complex: since it has a lot of many-ness, it contains many potential "idols." Sometimes this means that people give their all to another human being — for the kamikaze pilots who went on suicide missions during World War II, it was "emperor-ism." For others, idolatry can go in a more abstract direction, making racial identity, lustful pursuits, or devotion to an ideology their ultimate allegiance or organizing principle.

This way of understanding idolatrous patterns that came into being with the Fall is, of course, no new teaching. St. Augustine waxed eloquent on this subject already in the fourth century after Christ. In one of his works, he offers a rather elaborate typology of idolatries. Some people, he says, "worship the soul in place of the most high God," while others "slip further down and worship animals and even material things." Others direct their worship upward to "the heavenly

7. Robert N. Bellah et al., *Habits of the Heart: Individualism and Commitment in American Life* (Berkeley: University of California Press, 1985), 221.

bodies." And then there are those, he says, who "think themselves most religious" because they have chosen to "worship the whole created universe, that is, the world with all that is in it, and the life which inspires and animates it. . . . The whole of this together they think to be one great God, of whom all things are parts." Whatever people choose to worship, from the lowest to the highest beings, he observes, it is all idolatry, because "[t]hey have not known the author and maker of the universe."[8]

In making these idolatrous choices people are, of course, fixating on something that is a part of the good creation. Political parties and movements are worthy of our respect when they are kept in their place — in their proper sphere of life. What about racial or ethnic identity? That too is a good thing: "Black is beautiful" — and so is Czech, or Latino, or Japanese. Money and possessions, properly understood, are gifts from God. Freely chosen gender roles can be a helpful means for structuring our dates and marriages and families. Cheering for a favorite baseball team can be a healthy way of spending a leisurely evening.

All those good things become dangerous only when we make one or another of them the center of an "ism." Egotism. Totalitarianism. Ethnocentrism. Materialism. Sexism. Fanatical Dodger-ism. When these "isms" take hold of our hearts in fruitless attempts to organize all of life by directing our most basic loyalties to something creaturely, we have slipped into idolatry.

It is God in Christ alone who "sustains all things by his powerful word" (Hebrews 1:3). By directing our worship to-

---

8. Augustine, *Of True Religion*, trans. J. H. S. Burleigh (Washington: Henry Regnery Co., 1966), 65-66.

ward the true God, we thereby allow the "all things" simply to be what they are — the splendid many-ness in which God takes delight.

We can summarize Kuyper's overall advice on how to avoid idolatry with this maxim: *What the Creator wants us to keep apart, let no human being try to squeeze together.*

DON'T EVER TRY TO CHANGE GOD'S CREATIONS & ORDERS.

The Spheres

———— ∞∞∞ ————

"**S**phere sovereignty" is the English term used for Kuyper's Dutch phrase *(soevereiniteit in eigen kring)*. The Dutch here is a little difficult to translate literally, but it has the sense of each sphere having its own unique or separate character. Each cultural sphere has its own place in God's plan for the creation, and each is directly under the divine rule. This is the basic insight of his theory of sphere sovereignty.

What Kuyper meant by a "sphere" is pretty much what we have in mind when we talk about a person's "sphere of influence." It is an arena where interactions take place, and where some sort of authority is exercised.

Kuyper was never very precise as to what *counted* as a creational "sphere." He offers various lists. So if we are looking for precision in the exact number of spheres, we are not going to get much help from Kuyper. But that should not keep us from taking seriously the big theme that he is articulating. He is pointing us to some obvious patterns of cultural interaction — family life, business, art, the university, church, state — and he is saying that each of these is intended by God to do its own "thing"; each has a different role or "point" in God's design for his creation. The state should not control the arts, nor should universities (or seminaries!) see themselves primarily as businesses.

Here is how one Kuyperian scholar put it: "Each sphere has its own identity, its own unique task, its own God-given prerogatives. On each God has conferred its own peculiar right of existence and reason for existence."[1]

Kuyper meant, among other things, to counter the idea that such entities as the state or the family or the market system exist only because the state grants them the right to exist. Governments do not *grant* these rights; they are called to *recognize* rights. We have families and churches and economic systems because they are grounded in creation itself.

Furthermore, God has ordained that these diverse spheres have their own places in the creation because they fulfill different creational purposes. The point of creating or performing art is to display aesthetic excellence, while the point of science — a term which Kuyper uses broadly to cover all orderly intellectual investigation — is to advance the cause of knowledge. Economic activity aims at stewardship. Politics aims at justice.

Differing Exercises of Authority

Corresponding to these different "points" is a diversity of authority patterns. The way in which a parent exercises author-

1. Gordon J. Spykman, "Sphere Sovereignty in Calvin and the Calvinist Tradition," in David E. Holwerda, ed., *Exploring the Heritage of John Calvin* (Grand Rapids: Baker, 1976), 167.

ity over a child should be different from the way a manager exercises authority over staff, or a professor over students, or a coach over team players. This means too that the skills associated with a specific mode of authority do not automatically transfer to other spheres.

Imagine a woman and a man who are related in three different ways. She is the young man's mother. She is also an elder in the church where their family worships. And she is the academic dean at the university where her son serves on the faculty. Suppose, though, that the young man commits a serious crime — using, for example, a university computer for illicit sexual purposes. As his dean she will be required to fire him. As his church elder she might participate in a decision to place him under some form of ecclesiastical discipline — requiring, say, some special expression of penitence to God and to the community as a part of a process of spiritual restoration, and if he is not repentant, she may have to agree to a decision to excommunicate him from church membership. But as his mother she continues to love him unconditionally as a member of the family; she never entertains thoughts of "disowning" him as a son.

In each case her authority role is a different one, as is also the basis for her acceptance of him within each relationship. In the university she judges his fitness to remain a member of the community by some straightforwardly formal standards of vocational performance. In the church, she also enforces certain norms, but here with a pastoral openness to repentance and spiritual renewal. In the family, the ties go much deeper — so much so that the bond is not easily broken by either bad performance or unrepentant sin. In short, the authority exercised by a dean is different from that of an elder, and each differs from the parental role. And this is because families are families, churches are churches, and the academy is the academy. So if the young man were to complain to his mother, "How can you fire me from my teaching job? — I'm your *son*," he would be blurring the boundaries of the spheres.

Sphere Sovereignty and Subsidiarity

Kuyper's sphere sovereignty idea is often compared favorably to a similar notion that looms large in Roman Catholic thought: what the Catholics call "the principle of subsidiarity." On this view, "higher" structures should never do for "lower" ones what they can do for themselves. So national governments should not interfere unnecessarily with state governments, states with cities, cities with neighborhoods, neighborhoods with families, and so on.

The difference between subsidiarity and sphere sovereignty should be obvious from the examples I have listed. The subsidiarity idea focuses on the need for decentralizing authority within what Kuyper would see as a sovereign sphere. For him, the United States government and the Idaho government are both in the same sphere, politics, and he is focusing on the need to keep politics as such from interfering unnecessarily with, say, family or church.

That difference is a real one, but we should at least mention that Kuyper would also have some sympathy for the subsidiarity notion. Sometimes, for example, Catholic theologians use the subsidiarity idea to argue that a pope should not unnecessarily interfere with the work of a local bishop. And the fact is that Kuyper liked to make a parallel point about church life within his own Reformed tradition, where he constantly warned against the "hierarchical" heavy-handedness that shows up when national or regional church bodies interfere unnecessarily in the life of the local church. Kuyper's "localist" tendencies came through in his Stone Lecture on politics, where he says that "the social life of cities and villages" forms "a separate sphere of existence . . . which therefore must be autonomous."[2] So, while his sympathy for the "local" does not, strictly speaking, follow from his notion of sphere sovereignty (although he may even have merged the two himself on occasion), it is difficult to think that there is no spillover from Kuyper's prescriptions about relationships *among* the spheres to his views about relationships *within* the spheres.

2. Kuyper, *Lectures*, 96.

Cultural "Dykes and Dams"

———— ⊕⊕⊕ ————

James Hutton MacKay was a Scottish clergyman who spent six years, shortly after the turn of the twentieth century, serving in the Netherlands as a pastor to the English-speaking congregations in a couple of different Dutch towns. Soon after he returned to Scotland from his Dutch sojourn, he gave the Hastie Lectures at the University of Glasgow. These lectures, delivered in February 1911, dealt with nineteenth-century Dutch religious thought. In the course of describing some of the more orthodox thinkers of nineteenth-century Holland, MacKay offered these observations about the mental habits of the Dutch:

> They like to see things clearly, and to see them as they are — at least, as they seem to be to men of sound understanding. "We are a people of dykes and dams," a Dutch writer said recently, "both as to our land and our mental life." And Dr. Kuyper's often-quoted saying about the danger of "blurring the boundary lines" is characteristically Dutch. . . . Much, I believe, can be learned from a

people who have a remarkable gift of making distinctions, wrought into their nature, possibly, by many centuries of unrelaxing toil in making and holding that distinction between land and sea, which to them is a matter
of life and death.[1]

As we will see, there certainly are a lot of "dykes and dams"
in Kuyper's theology of culture. And the theological geogra-
phy of those boundary-markers is sketched out in what is ar-
guably his most distinctive teaching, his theory of "sphere
sovereignty."

Our sinful tendency to squeeze things together is what led
Kuyper to worry about — to quote the title of another of his essays — "the blurring of the boundaries."[2] Obviously the Fall
itself was a blurring of the most basic boundary. Human beings wanted to be their own gods, and in doing so were seeking to eliminate that huge gap between Creator and creature.

All the other, more specific forms of idolatry begin with
that fundamental blurring attempt. Sometimes we try to
bring the divine down to earth by absorbing God into nature.
This results in all the varieties of naturalism, a denial of anything that transcends the world of nature. At other times we
attempt to bring ourselves (and sometimes everything else
along with us!) into the realm of the divine. We see this in the
sort of "transcendental humanism" of Ralph Waldo Emerson
and, more recently, the New Age movement, in which people
attempt a "divinization" of our finite human reality by search-
ing for "higher forms of consciousness."

1. James Hutton MacKay, *Religious Thought in Holland during the Nine-
teenth Century* (New York: Hodder & Stoughton, 1911), p. 10.
2. Abraham Kuyper, "The Blurring of the Boundaries," in Bratt, *Abraham Kuyper: A Centennial Reader,* 363-402.

Kuyper was concerned about these patterns. His concern to protect the fundamental distinction between the Creator and the creaturely shows up in many areas of his thought. In his theology of culture in particular he was convinced that when we lose sight of that important distinction, we immediately run the risk of blurring the boundary lines that separate the diverse created spheres of human interaction.

Patrolling the Boundaries

During the years that I have been teaching about culture and related issues, both in college and seminary classes, I have regularly included lectures on Abraham Kuyper's thought, often requiring my students to read the 1898 Stone Lectures. In my class discussions I have spent considerable time talking about his theory of "sphere sovereignty." A student in one of my Calvin College classes apparently had paid no attention to what went on in that part of the course. But this did not keep him from offering a rather bold account of what he imagined that Kuyper might say on the subject. In response to a question on the final examination inviting students to reflect critically on a major theme in Kuyper's social thought, this young man gave a summary of what he took to be Kuyper's espousal of "*spear* sovereignty." As a Calvinist, this student opined, Kuyper believed that governments have the power of the sword. Sinful people will never do anything good unless they have the threat of punishment held over their heads, as symbolized by a spear. So, the student argued, Kuyper believed that human society could only be held together by this fear. Thus, in a sinful world, the governmental "spear" must be sovereign.

While the student completely missed the point about Kuyper's *sphere* sovereignty teaching, I gave him some credit for his exercise in creative imagining. Furthermore, his brief account of the nature of political authority did bear some clear traces of things he had learned from his Calvinist upbringing. Romans 13, where the Apostle Paul talks about civil government's God-ordained power of the sword, has been a key text for the followers of John Calvin in their portrayal of the role of government — to the point that a slightly expanded paraphrase of that biblical passage has sometimes sufficed as a way of stating *the* Christian perspective on political life.

Kuyper's own views on political authority followed this general Calvinist line. But in spelling out his thoughts on sphere sovereignty, Kuyper was insisting that we cannot stop at talking about the state's God-given authority. He wanted to view political authority in a larger context, portraying the state's role against the background of a larger tapestry of human interaction. While the authority of government looms large in human affairs, we must view political life as only one of many cultural spheres. An important sphere, to be sure. But still — only one among many.

The need to keep government in its proper place is a topic that Kuyper addressed with considerable passion in his Stone Lecture on politics. The creation order, he argued, displays a rich variety of cultural spheres. Since all of these spheres have the same origin in "the divine mandate," political authority must respect the fact that each of the other spheres has its own integrity. ("Neither the life of science nor of art, nor of agriculture, nor of industry, nor of commerce, nor of navigation, nor of the family, nor of human relationship may be coerced to suit itself to the grace of government," says Kuyper.) "The State may never become an octopus, which stifles the whole of life." Then, abruptly switching from an aquatic to a botanic metaphor, he continues: political government "must occupy its own place, on its own root, among all the others trees of the forest, and thus it has to honor and maintain every form of life which grows independently in its own sacred autonomy."[3]

A Government's "Right and Duty"

At first glance, the octopus and tree references might seem to support the sort of "hands off" talk that we often hear these days from opponents of "big government." And, to be sure, Kuyper does lean somewhat in that direction. In employing the aquatic and botanic images he is obviously concerned to keep the government from undue intrusion in the affairs of the other spheres. But the key term here is *undue*.

Having used the metaphors of the tree whose roots spread too far and the grasping octopus, Kuyper quickly goes on to ask: "Does this mean that the government has no right *whatever* of interference in these autonomous spheres of life?" And his answer is: "Not at all." Government, he explains, has a "threefold right and duty": first, to adjudicate disputes between spheres, "compel[ling] mutual regard for the boundary-lines of each"; second, to defend the weak against the strong within each sphere; third, to exercise the coercive power necessary to guarantee that citizens "bear *personal* and *financial* burdens for the maintenance of the natural unity of the State."[4]

3. Kuyper, *Lectures,* 96-97.
4. Kuyper, *Lectures,* 97.

WONDER

Kuyper's three qualifications here are significant ones. Note that they not only suggest what governments *may* do; they point to what a state *must do.* And in this regard Kuyper does actually work with a kind of "spear sovereignty" notion. Government has a special role to play among the spheres, seeing to it — even if it has to threaten punishment in doing so — that the relationships among and within the spheres are properly ordered. And this ordering function is an active one. Indeed, as we will see now, one can make room, given the way Kuyper actually states his three qualifications, for a fairly energetic interventionist pattern for governments.

The first function that Kuyper mentions in specifying government's "threefold right and duty" is the patrolling of the boundaries between the spheres, in order to be sure that they do not get blurred — and in order to do something about it when that blurring actually takes place, as it so often does in *inter*-sphere boundary disputes. Suppose, for example, that a campus religious group protests a decision by public university authorities to refuse the group's application to use a classroom for a student Bible study gathering. This is an obvious case in which a government might well step in to settle the dispute.

There are other, more subtle, claims of alleged boundary violation that could also require government intervention. Suppose, for example, that parents want limits placed on TV advertising of fast-food products during times when children are most likely to be watching programs, on the grounds that such messages invade the home with propagandizing on behalf of poor nutrition. Or maybe homosexual organizations will claim that churches use their theology regarding sexuality to promote discriminatory attitudes in the larger public arena towards gay men and lesbians. While there is nothing in Kuyper's formulation that tells us *how* the government ought to decide in such cases, he does seem to imply that the government could have a proper boundary-clarifying role to play in these kinds of situations.

Kuyper's second qualification about the rights and duties of the state has to do with conflicts that can emerge *within* the spheres: government is obliged to protect the weak from the strong within each sphere. Here again, there are obvious cases: governments may, for example, intervene in families where spousal or child abuse occurs, or in manufacturing firms where there are oppressive workplace conditions. But this qualification can also be interpreted to include less overt patterns of perceived harm, of the sort frequently associated these days with the more subtle varieties of sexual harassment.

Kuyper's third qualification has to do with what we might think of as *trans*-spherical patterns — things that the government must take responsibility for because they affect multiple spheres. His concern here can be illustrated with a simple example: public thoroughfares. Sidewalks, bike paths, streets, roads, and highways are used to conduct the affairs of a wide variety of spheres. Families pile into their vans to head for picnics. Heads of state travel to ceremonies in motorcades. Business leaders take cabs to meetings. Team players are bussed to a stadium. Students ride their bicycles to school. Worshipers walk to churches, synagogues, and mosques.

These thoroughfares serve all the spheres, and everyone, regardless of status in a particular sphere, has an interest in the maintenance of appropriate patterns of transport. It is the task of the state to see to it that we all do our part to maintain a good physical infrastructure.

Concern for the Poor

In 1891 Kuyper delivered a lengthy address to a "Christian Social Congress" in the Netherlands, translated into English as a short book, *Christianity and the Class Struggle.* It provides an interesting case study in Kuyper's views about addressing issues of poverty.

In dealing with the issues of economics, Kuyper makes it clear to his audience that he has no strong affinities to socialism. He strongly condemns the way socialists have often appealed to the example of Jesus, reinforcing that "mistaken conviction" that Jesus' expressions of concern for the needy have any link to the kind of economic theory advocated by socialism.

This is not to deny, Kuyper says, that the Bible does take economic injustice to be a serious offense to God. In fact, anyone who happened upon what the Apostle James writes on the subject — for example, James's warning that the rich will "weep and howl for [their] miseries that shall come upon [them]" for underpaying their laborers — would understandably "brand [James] as a crypto-socialist."[5]

The basic error of socialism as Kuyper sees it, though, is that it pits the poor against the rich. He points to Jesus' admonition to the poor person not to constantly be asking "what shall we eat, and what shall we drink, and wherewithal shall we be clothed? For all these things the Gentiles seek." Instead we are all to seek first God's Kingdom (Matthew 6:31-33). This appeal, says Kuyper, is a divine requirement that "simultaneously for both sides, rich and poor, cuts to the root of sin in

5. Abraham Kuyper, *Christianity and the Class Struggle,* trans. Dirk Jellema (Grand Rapids: Piet Hein Publishers, 1950), 23, n. 7.

our human heart."[6] Indeed, he says, it is important for all Christians to keep in mind that "[i]n every Lord's Prayer, the poor man prays *for the rich* that God may give him his bread for that day, and the rich prays it for the poor. Nowhere in this prayer is there a *my* or an *I;* but always a *we* and *us.*"[7]

Having emphasized our shared sinfulness and our shared concern for each other, however, Kuyper also notes that while "Jesus flattered no one, neither rich or poor, but put both in their place," we can still see "that Scripture, when it corrects the poor, does so much more tenderly and gently; and in contrast, when it calls the rich to account, uses much harsher words."[8] In his earthly ministry, Kuyper insists, Jesus, like the Old Testament prophets, "invariably took sides against those who were powerful and living in luxury, and *for* the suffering and oppressed."[9]

When he talks about solutions to the problems of poverty, Kuyper explicitly rejected state-administered welfare programs. We "should not seek salvation in *monetary* help from the State." That "weakens our national strength," he says. "The help the State must give is *better legislation.*"[10] This legislation should aim at strengthening the patterns of work in various spheres, including giving an effective voice to organized labor.[11] And the motivation to assist the poor must come from within those other spheres, with a special obligation for "deeds of love" from the Christian community.[12]

6. Kuyper, *Christianity and the Class Struggle,* 29.

7. Kuyper, *Christianity and the Class Struggle,* 27.

8. Kuyper, *Christianity and the Class Struggle,* 29, n. 13.

9. Kuyper, *Christianity and the Class Struggle,* 50.

10. Kuyper, *Christianity and the Class Struggle,* 57, n. 40.

11. Kuyper, *Christianity and the Class Struggle,* 58.

12. Kuyper, *Christianity and the Class Struggle,* 62.

While Kuyper rejects government financial assistance to the poor as a matter of principle, however, he is willing to grant an exception. "It is perfectly true," he says, "that if no help is forthcoming from elsewhere the State *must help*. We may let no one starve from hunger, so long as bread lies molding in so many cupboards. And also, when the State intervenes, it must do so *quickly and sufficiently.*"

Here again, while Kuyper is intent upon keeping the state in its proper place, he also insists that a government has both a right *and* a duty to reach *from* that place into the other spheres, regulating inter-, intra-, and trans-spherical patterns. One can surely raise questions about how often and how far a government may reach in pursuing these obligations. Those are good and important questions. But Kuyper point clearly to the need to deal with those questions within a framework that acknowledges a proper role for government in seeing to it that the spheres co-exist in a relatively stable and healthy manner.

"Placing" Kuyper Politically

———— ∞∞∞ ————

It is difficult to read what Kuyper says about the proper functions of the state without trying to "place" him with reference to contemporary debates. Given the kinds of things Kuyper said in his nineteenth-century context, where would he locate himself today on the "liberal" to "conservative" spectrum of views in the twenty-first century?

For many of us who take his views on political matters seriously, this is no question of idle speculation. It is a question about *us*. And the question — about Kuyper himself and about those of us who look to his views for contemporary guidance — is difficult to answer clearly.

The left-versus-right dilemma is not unique to Kuyperians. It is a problem for many evangelicals these days. We care about the poor. We are often critical of the military actions taken by our governments. We support environmentalist policies. We oppose racism and gender discrimination.

But we often find ourselves aligning ourselves with concerns that get expressed on the right. We worry about the sexual trends in our society. We oppose abortion-on-demand. We speak out against the naturalistic and secularist biases that often seem to rule the day in the media and the world of education.

Again, that is true for many evangelicals — Mennonites, Baptists, Pentecostals, Wesleyans — as well as friends in the Catholic community. But for some of us, the Kuyperian view of the role of the state also figures into the way we see many of these topics.

A Third Way

⟨⟨⟨∞⟩⟩⟩

To get at the basic thrust of Kuyper's sphere sovereignty idea, it is helpful to see how he saw his overall perspective on God's relationship to the various spheres of cultural life as posing an alternative to two competing pictures. The first competing picture is what Kuyper saw as the church-controlled culture of the medieval period, in which ecclesiastical authority claimed the right (even though it did not always exercise the right) to give "Christian" direction to various spheres of interaction: family life, the arts, politics, economic activity, and so on. The second is the secularist viewpoint that took hold in Western culture as a reaction against the church's attempts to exercise control over all of cultural life.

For Kuyper, each of these two models embodied both a positive insight and a fundamental error. The medieval perspective rightly saw that God's rule must be acknowledged over all spheres of human activity. Its mistake was investing the church with the power to mediate that rule. Here is the picture:

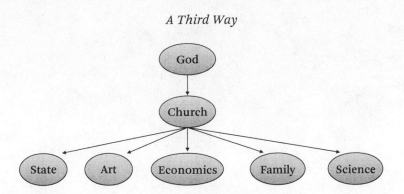

The secularist perspective rightly wants to liberate these spheres from the church's control. Where it goes wrong is in its insistence that to do so is also to take them out from under the rule of God. If there is a God, the secularists have said, he can have the church — but we will liberate everything else from divine control.

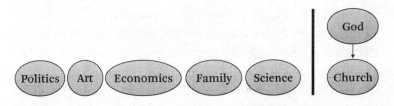

Kuyper's own view — his alternative to these other two pictures — was nicely captured by his "not one square inch" manifesto. God's sovereign rule extends over all of our lives. All of the cultural spheres are in place — to use a favorite Kuyperian phrase — *coram deo,* before the face of God.

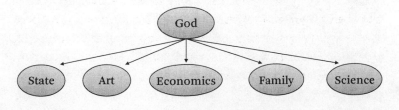

The great error of unbelief, then, is the pretense that we are on our own, that we are not accountable to our Maker for anything that we do. The Christian community must live out its calling in the conscious recognition that secularism is false.

For Kuyper, this meant that Christians must form collective entities within each of the spheres in order to make our confession of God's sovereignty concrete: art guilds, political parties, farmers' federations, laborers' associations.

The major academic institution founded by Kuyper provides a helpful example of how his viewpoint worked out in practical life. He gave it the name *Vrije Universiteit* — "Free University" — because he wanted it to be *free* from both ecclesiastical and political control. The university's Christian identity was to be guaranteed by "Reformed principles" for academic life that were to be implemented and monitored by a Christian association that was independent of both church and state.

"Mediating Structures"

A number of North American social critics have emphasized in recent years the important role that a wide variety of social arrangements and associations play in providing a buffer between the individual and the state. The sociologist Peter Berger made that case already in the 1970s, when he complained that scholars who study our societal patterns often fail to give proper attention to what he labeled "mediating structures." If we are to avoid the twin evils of individualism on the one hand and statism — in which governments exercise totalitarian control — on the other, he argued, we must pay attention to the character-forming role of families, neighborhood organizations, youth clubs, service groups, churches and synagogues, and the like.[1]

In more recent decades, an important group of scholars have taken up that topic with considerable enthusiasm, studying the patterns of "civil society." A prominent case in point is the work of Harvard political scientist Robert Putnam. In a much-discussed 1993 essay, "Bowling Alone," and in a 2001 book with the same title,[2] Putnam bemoaned the decline of participation in "voluntary societies" in North American culture. His title, for example, is a reference to the fact that while more Americans are bowling than ever before, fewer people are joining bowling leagues than in the past. When people "bowl alone," they do not build social networks — eating and drinking together — during their bowling activities, and there is a significant loss, Putnam argues, in the "social capital" that is associated with camaraderie and team spirit. The decline in these types of social bonds means that individuals do not develop the qualities of public character that are the preconditions for a healthy participation in civil society. When this pattern prevails, the dangers posed by Berger's individualism-or-statism alternatives are acute.

On a practical level, this fits nicely with some of Kuyper's own concerns. But Kuyper wanted to probe more deeply than simply insisting that a healthy society should be sure to foster a lot of voluntary associations. He wanted to see how these

1. Peter Berger, *Facing Up to Modernity: Excursions in Society, Politics and Religion* (New York: Basic Books, 1977), 140.

2. Robert Putnam, "Bowling Alone," *Journal of Democracy* 6:1 (January 1995), 65-78; for the book version see Robert Putnam, *Bowling Alone: The Collapse and Revival of American Community* (New York: Simon and Schuster, 2000).

patterns of social interaction fit into God's creating designs for human life. And he was especially interested in the kinds of social relationships that we can find in the basic spheres of cultural life that are such an important part of God's ordering of the creation.

In thinking about things on this deeper level, Kuyper wanted to be sure that we keep the very basic differences among these created spheres in mind. To talk simply about "civil society" is to ignore the rich diversity of the created spheres. Families are different than churches. Art guilds are different than groups of scientists working on a common project. Businesses are different than academic communities. These various unique groupings were important for him, not just because they help to curb the power of the state to control our sense of identity, but because they also display diverse patterns of human interaction that God wanted to be a part of the developing of creation. Whether it is good to have Rotary Clubs and parent-teacher associations is not as important a question for Kuyper as whether art and religion and business and family life, as fundamental spheres of cultural interaction, are each granted their allotted place in the God-ordained scheme of things.

Spheres in the Bible?

———— ∞∞∞ ————

Here is a big question I often get asked by people who are just getting familiar with Kuyper on the spheres: *Is this idea biblical?* Can the ideas associated with sphere sovereignty in any way be thought of as taught in the Scriptures? Granted, Kuyper is quite eloquent in insisting that God built a diversity of cultural spheres into his design for the creation. But where would we look in the Bible for the biblical *basis* for this teaching?

While we could wish that Kuyper and his followers said more on this topic, there are occasional references to what they apparently view as a biblical grounding for the sphere sovereignty idea. As already shown, Kuyper does like to appeal to the line in the Genesis story that says that plants and animals were created "after their own kind." Kuyper's younger colleague Herman Bavinck (an important theological figure in his own right) makes the connection here between the creation of the animals as unique kinds and a variety of creational spheres. "Just as creatures received a nature of their own in creation and differ among themselves," he ar-

gues, "so there is a difference in the laws" to which those creatures must conform in their various functions. And after observing that the "laws and relations differ in every sphere,"
Bavinck immediately illustrates the variety of those spheres:
"the physical and the psychological, the intellectual and the
ethical, the family and society, science and art, the kingdoms
of earth and the kingdom of heaven."[1]

Separation of Powers

Kuyper himself provides the outline of an even larger biblically
related rationale for sphere sovereignty when he poses the
question in his address at the founding of the Free University
of "whether 'sphere sovereignty' is derived from the heart of
Scripture and from the treasury of Reformed life." Kuyper explains what gave rise to this conception in his thinking:

> Should anyone ask whether "sphere sovereignty" is
> really derived from the heart of Scripture and the trea-
> sury of Reformed life, I would entreat him first of all to
> plumb the depths of the organic *faith principle* in Scrip-
> ture, further to note Hebron's tribal law for David's coro-
> nation, to notice Elijah's resistance to Ahab's tyranny,
> the disciples' refusal to yield to Jerusalem's police regu-
> lations, and, not least, to listen to their Lord's maxim
> concerning what is God's and what is Caesar's. As to Re-
> formed life, don't you know about Calvin's "lesser mag-
> istrates"? Isn't sphere sovereignty the basis for the en-

1. Herman Bavinck, *Reformed Dogmatics,* Vol. 2: *God and Creation,*
trans. John Vriend (Grand Rapids: Baker Academic, 2004), 610.

tire presbyterian church order? Did not almost all Reformed nations incline toward a confederative form of government? Are not civil liberties most luxuriantly developed in Reformed lands? Can it be denied that domestic peace, decentralization, and municipal autonomy are best guaranteed even today among the heirs of Calvin?[2]

Kuyper loads a variety of biblical and historical examples into that paragraph, and one could write a long essay explaining what he has in mind with each example. It should at least be obvious, though, that what they all have in common is this: each example illustrates in one way or another the separation of powers: a prophet refusing to obey a king, the apostles refusing to respect a police order to stop preaching, and so on.

Is any of that convincing as a rationale for sphere sovereignty? In one sense, obviously, it is not. It is one thing to note, in the spirit of Kuyper's list of examples, that God saw to it that the separate offices of prophet, priest, and king were distinguished in the life of ancient Israel, or that presbyterian polity assigns different functions to pastors, elders, and deacons. But it is another thing to insist that we can look to the Bible for confirmation that God shaped the world in such a way that, say, universities would have different creational mandates than churches.

Kuyper, Bavinck, and others do make some significant "leaps" when they talk about sphere sovereignty as a biblical teaching. Not everyone will be convinced that we can go from rather straightforward paraphrases of biblical references to

2. Kuyper, "Sphere Sovereignty," in Bratt, *Abraham Kuyper: A Centennial Reader,* 480-81.

planets, plants, and the like, to more general statements about a lawful order that those specific created things must obey — and then to an even more general account of created spheres.

A Creative Leap

Yes, there certainly are some leaps in all of that. But at least two points have to be made in defense of what Kuyper and Bavinck are doing. One is that they are engaged in the kind of intellectual activity that gives life to much good theological reflection. This is the kind of thing that theologians — really good theologians — do. They go beyond the explicit statements of Scripture to explore larger patterns of coherence that can shed light on the patterns and implications of what the Bible explicitly says. That's precisely the kind of thing that happens when theologians write treatises on the Trinity, or when they spell out what they see as a biblically faithful understanding of the church.

The second point in defense of the Kuyperian view is that there is a "fit" of sorts between the actual biblical passages Kuyper and Bavinck allude to and the more speculative claims that they make. The Bible does address in very specific ways how God shapes and governs the creation. What Kuyper and Bavinck are doing is to try to catch the spirit of those specific references in order to talk in more general terms and categories about how God structures and orders created life.

Much the same can be said for the way Kuyper moves from actual biblical examples of the separation of powers to more general claims about God's desire to draw clear lines of separation among the societal spheres. To be sure, Kuyper is making a leap of sorts. But in doing so Kuyper is asking us to consider the possibility that these particular examples illustrate a more general divine interest in the separation of powers, by viewing these separations as built into the very fabric of creation itself.

Politics and Creation

⸻ ◈ ⸻

The basic cultural spheres have been, for Kuyper, "there" from the beginning. They are somehow "contained in" the creation. In saying that kind of thing, Kuyper is once again going beyond the explicit biblical data. It's not like we read the Bible saying that God proclaimed, "Let there be art! Let there be economics! Let there be politics!" So what does it mean to say that these were a part of the original creational design?

The Kuyperian insistence that the political sphere was a part of the creational design is especially interesting in this regard. Like any Calvinist, Kuyper insisted that under sinful conditions governments have a God-ordained ministry of the sword. In a fallen world political authority has a remedial function. For one thing it holds our sinful impulses in check with the threat of punishment. I might be inclined to drive ten miles per hour over the speed limit, but the awareness that I might have to pay a fine if caught by a patrol car keeps me in line.

But government also *exercises* the ministry of the sword. It doesn't just threaten punishment — sometimes it actually punishes. The police and military arms of the state are empowered to apprehend criminals and administer justice by the use of force. Thus the Apostle's admonition: "if you do what is wrong, you should be afraid, for the authority does not bear the sword in vain! It is the servant of God to execute wrath on the wrongdoer" (Romans 13:4).

Kuyper was not content, however, to restrict the role of government in God's plan simply to a post-Fall function. He insisted that what we experience as political authority under fallen conditions is a manifestation of something that was already implicit in the original creation design. Kuyper argued in his Stone Lecture on politics that even if the Fall had not occurred there would have developed a need for government. Political authority in an unfallen world would not have taken the form of coercive nation-states; rather there would have emerged "one organic world-empire, with God as its King; exactly what is prophesied for the future which awaits us, when all sin shall have disappeared."[1] Here government is not fundamentally a remedial response to human perversity, but a natural provision for regulating — "ordering" — the complexity of created cultural life.

A Contrary-to-Fact Exercise

Kuyper liked to think about what things would be like in the creation if the Fall had not occurred. This obviously strikes some as highly speculative. And in an important sense it is an exercise in speculation. For those of us, though, who find biblically-inspired imaginative proposals to be useful theological exercises, this is not necessarily a bad thing.

1. Kuyper, *Lectures,* 92.

There is a helpful parallel to be drawn here to a strategy that some historians have been employing recently in attempting to understand certain historical developments. A good place to see this strategy at work is a volume of essays authored by some well-known historians, exploring "what might have been" in American history.[2] The scholars ask what might have happened if the Mayflower had run into weather that brought it to Virginia rather than Plymouth Rock. And what if General Lee had won the Battle of Gettysburg? And what if the Japanese had not bombed Pearl Harbor? The posing of "contrary-to-fact" questions of this sort can shed some light for our understanding of the contemporary world.

When Kuyper speculates about political systems without the Fall, he means to illuminate something important about the need for order in human affairs. Suppose a tuba player who lives in an apartment complex wants to practice on a daily basis at the same time as a neighbor puts her children down for a nap. Neither is motivated by sinful impulses — they simply have different desires that are in themselves quite legitimate. The tuba player wants to be a good musician and the woman wants to be a good parent.

Or think about traffic patterns. Even sinless people would have to agree about which side of the road they would use when driving their cars. Thus the need for the regulation of group activities, even when it is not necessary to reinforce such regulative activity with coercive threats.

It is with these kinds of considerations in mind that

2. Robert Cowley, ed., *What Ifs? of American History: Eminent Historians Imagine What Might Have Been* (New York: Berkley Books, 2003). The "What If?" approach to major historical events has also produced a genre of "alternative history" novels: Harry Turtledove's Civil War novels are prominent in this category.

Kuyper says that even if the Fall had not occurred we would still need some kind of regulative governing function. To offer an effective rebuttal to that line of argument, it is not sufficient simply to reject the use of the counterfactual as such; rather it is necessary to show that there is something conceptually implausible about what the counterfactual claim is meant to illustrate — namely, the idea of a political order that regulates life in an unfallen world.

"Life-Giving" Politics

During the 1970s, I attended a gathering that focused on "radical discipleship," and one of the speakers kept describing the United States as given over to "the way of death." His primary example, of course, was the war being waged in Vietnam — this was a group that was very critical of that military operation. He formulated his case theologically by citing William Stringfellow's argument, quite popular at the time, that the United States was the present-day manifestation of the biblical portrayal of fallen Babylon.[3]

As I listened, I was struck by the gap between this unnuanced rhetorical depiction of the American political system as given over to death dealing and my own experience that very week of accompanying our son on his way to school. He had just started kindergarten, and his daily walk to school followed a path through many blocks in the inner city. As I took the journey with him, I was especially aware, as a parent concerned for the safety of our son, of the places where there

---

3. Cf. William Stringfellow, *An Ethics for Christians and Other Aliens in a Strange Land* (Waco: Word Publishing Company, 1973).

were traffic lights and stop signs. Approaching the school, I overheard two teachers mention a fire-safety inspection that the city had conducted the day before. Later, as I drove during the noon hour to the campus where I was teaching, I passed another school where a uniformed crossing guard was taking children by the hand to lead them across the street.

These things that I had taken special notice of as a concerned parent — traffic signals, stop signs, speed limits, crossing guards — struck me as life-promoting services provided by the government. I thanked the Lord for them. In the light of those services, the passionate denunciation of "the American system" as given over to "a way of death" was evidence of a theological myopia.

My uneasiness with that kind of perspective was grounded in what I am presenting here as a very basic Kuyperian impulse: there is something about government, when it is functioning properly, that fits nicely into God's basic creating design for human life.

The Church's Place

———✸———

Precisely because governments play an important role in human life they are also dangerous entities. They can so easily try to reach beyond their proper place in the created scheme of things — that's the point of Kuyper's "grasping" images of the octopus and tree roots. And we have to be very clear about the proper bounds of government, since in any nation there can be only one of them. *ONE GOVERNMENT IN EVERY COUNTRY, BUT THERE CAN BE MANY CHURCHES NOT ONLY ONE.*

Not so with churches. To be sure, there are situations where a church — or some other organized religious body — aligns itself so closely with political power that there is only one "established" church. When that happens, the two kinds of authority are difficult to untangle. But where that exists in our own day it is viewed by many as an unfortunate relic of the past.

We already saw that Kuyper was strongly in favor of churchly "pluriformity." He was convinced that — even though it took a while to develop — the Reformation had set in motion an impulse that encouraged the breaking of the "one Church into fragments," resulting in "a rich variety of all manner of church formations."[1]

Kuyper's enthusiasm for churchly "fragments" was partly due to his love of "many-ness" in general. But there was more to it than that. He did not want the church to see itself as the God-ordained authority over the other cultural spheres. He was convinced that the medieval church had erred in this regard. It saw itself as mediating God's will to the other spheres.

Kuyper rejected that idea. Families, banks, university faculties, political parties, *and the church* — all of these exist, on Kuyper's view, *coram deo,* directly before the face of God. The church has no business telling artists how to do their creative work, or business people how to go about their economic activity, or farmers how to raise their crops. Having many churches, then, is a way of keeping any one church from overreaching.

Kuyper's convictions on this subject led him to a very personal decision at one point in his career. He had started off his life as a leader as an ordained Dutch Reformed minister. But when he became active in politics, seeking election in the Dutch parliament, he gave up his ordination. From that point on he was a member of the laity. This decision was motivated in large part by his deep opposition to even the appearance of using the mantle of ecclesiastical office to influence life in another sphere. He wanted to make it clear that the exercise of authority within political life is different than the exercise of authority in the church. The two spheres have different assignments in the ordering of created life.

1. Kuyper, *Lectures,* 101.

Church and Kingdom

Kuyper makes much of the fact that the Kingdom of Christ is much bigger than the institutional church. The Kingdom is that broad range of reality over which Christ rules. Actually, Christ's Kingdom is the whole cosmos — remember Kuyper's manifesto about every square inch of the creation belonging to Jesus. But in a more focused sense — the sense we will be assuming here — the Kingdom covers all of those areas of reality where Christ's rule is *acknowledged* by those who work to make that rule visible.

The institutional church is certainly an important part of Christ's Kingdom. It is where we as believers gather to worship — where we are shaped by the preaching of the Word, by participation in sacraments, by instruction in the church's traditions and teachings, and by less formal patterns of fellowship. In the life of the institutional church, believers regularly acknowledge the authority of Jesus Christ over their daily lives.

But the church is only one part of the Kingdom. And it is no trivial thing to point that out. I once heard a prominent pastor complain from the pulpit about lay people — he used the example of Christians in the business community — who don't give enough of their time to church activities. This is how he put it: "These folks work all day at their marketplace jobs, and then they go home and watch television. Other than coming to Sunday services," he said, "they don't seem to care about Kingdom activities!"

Kuyper would have been horrified by that statement — as I was. The pastor was equating church and Kingdom, as if the two terms were interchangeable. Kuyper would urge business people to see their places of work as providing important opportunities for Kingdom service.

CHURCH

The institutional church is the entity that meets regularly MATTERS A LOT for what we normally think of as churchly activities — the essential ones being worship (preaching and sacraments), catchesis (educating members in the teachings and history of THEIR the Christian faith), and outreach (sponsoring programs of DIFFERENCE evangelism, missions, and charity). The church, then, occupies a specific sphere, an area of cultural activity that exists alongside other spheres.

KINGDOM The Kingdom, on the other hand, encompasses the believing community in all of its complex life of participation in a variety of spheres. Wherever followers of Christ are attempting to glorify God in one or another sphere of cultural interaction, they are engaged in Kingdom activity: a Christian art guild gathered for obedience in the sphere of the arts; a Christian farmers' group gathered for obedience in the sphere of agriculture; a Christian college or university gathered for obedience in the world of teaching and research. And so on. It is all the Kingdom.

Note that I use the word "gathered" in these examples. That is important for understanding Kuyper. It wasn't enough for him that Christians to engage in cultural activity on an individual basis. We all need to seek communal discernment for various areas of cultural life. So the believing community must form sub-communities that focus on obedience to the will of God for the various cultural spheres. The church, for Kuyper, is one of many Christian sub-communities.

Churchly "Expertise"

It isn't difficult to think of a compelling practical reason for limiting the role of the institutional church in the way that

Kuyper insists. Church leaders simply do not have the expertise to deal with all of the complexities of our callings in various spheres of cultural life. They cannot prescribe the details of government legislation, evaluation of art, or basketball strategies.

As someone involved on a daily basis in educating people for church-related ministries, I am very aware of the challenges in this area. Pastoral ministry has become much more complex in recent decades. In the congregations where I grew up as a pastor's son, my dad prepared sermons, led worship, visited the sick, and conducted weddings and funerals. He knew nothing about staff ministries with "executive pastors" and "singles' ministries," nor would he ever have thought to go to a seminar on "conflict management."

In present-day seminaries we offer courses in all sorts of areas of specialized ministries. And lay leaders are frequently telling us we need to do a better job of producing pastors who are better prepared to deal with budgets, lead meetings, and engage in strategic planning. It is too much to expect that we would also feel obligated to equip pastors to provide expert guidance to artists, surgeons, restaurateurs, software developers, farmers, or hedge-fund managers.

Kuyper's concept of the calling of the institutional church makes good sense in this context. What people need from the church is what is essential: the gospel and the way it sets forth the basic patterns for living the Christian life. Whether Christians happen to spend most of their time in our homes or in the marketplace, we need to know what is central to the biblical message and the Christian tradition, and we must be nurtured in our growth in the faith by Christian fellowship, spiritual formation, and the sacraments. For the church to be faithful in a changing world, performing these tasks well is challenge enough.

The Antithesis

———— ∞∞∞ ————

C alvinists have a reputation for harboring rather pessimistic views about fallen human nature. And that reputation is well deserved. When God saves us, says John Calvin, he brings about a fundamental transformation in our inner being, from "an evil will to a good will." Any of the original light of the original creation that remains in fallen humanness is nonetheless so "choked with dense ignorance . . . that it cannot come forth effectively."[1] The seemingly virtuous traits that we observe in unredeemed lives are, he says, "so sullied that before God they lose all favor," so that anything in them "that appears praiseworthy must be considered worthless."[2]

The same holds more specifically for the sinful intellect. The mind of fallen human beings, Calvin insists, simply "wanders through various errors and stumbles repeatedly, as if it were groping in the darkness. . . . Thus it betrays how inca-

1. John Calvin, *Institutes of the Christian Religion,* ed. John T. McNeill, trans. Ford Lewis Battles (Philadelphia: Westminster Press, 1960), II: 2, 12, 270.

2. Calvin, *Institutes,* II: 3, 4, 294.

pable it is of seeking and finding truth."[3] Citing the Apostle Paul in Ephesians 2, Calvin describes the difference between fallen Adam and the way of Christ in terms of "an antithesis"[4] — a radical opposition between two very different realities.

Different "Peoples," Different "Minds"

Kuyper took this term "antithesis" and turned it into a prominent feature of his thought. He insisted on the reality of what he referred to frequently as "*the* antithesis," the basic opposition that he saw as holding between the patterns of human life and thought in its fallenness and that which God intends for the life and thought of the redeemed community. This had important implications for his view of, for example, the intellectual life. One of Kuyper's much-quoted lines goes like this: "the fact that there are two kinds of *people* [redeemed and unredeemed] occasions of necessity the fact of two kinds of human life and *consciousness* of life, and of two kinds of *science*."[5]

When Kuyper refers to "science" he often means something more than what we associate with the natural and social sciences. From *scio*, "science" can mean the broad patterns of "knowing." Earlier I mentioned Kuyper's insistence that the sin of the Fall was a turning of the will — sinful human beings turn away from doing all to the glory of God to the placing of ultimate trust in something less than the true Creator of all things. This affects our ways of "knowing." We no longer grasp and integrate things in appropriate ways. Our "world

3. Calvin, *Institutes,* II: 2, 12, 270-71.
4. Calvin, *Institutes,* II: 3, 4, 294.
5. Abraham Kuyper, *Principles of Sacred Theology,* trans. J. Hendrik De Vries (Grand Rapids: Eerdmans, 1954), 154 (emphasis his).

and life view" — a favorite Kuyperian phrase — is shaped and guided by our rebellious spirits. It is only when God redirects our wills back toward him that we can begin to correct our ways of knowing.

This way of seeing things is what led Kuyper to establish his Free University. He wanted an academic community in which all areas of intellectual pursuit could be consciously pursued by hearts and minds devoted to honoring God in all things. Our scholarly lives will be different if we take seriously the idea that we live in a universe created by God, and that as human beings we are fashioned in the image and likeness of the divine.

The Last Word?

That emphasis on an antithesis between regenerate and unregenerate life and thought makes good theological sense to Calvinists. And some followers of John Calvin are content to let the antithesis be the last word on the question of how we are to understand the implications of the insistence on the reality of "two kinds of people" in the world. This attitude shows up in the very practical sort of Christianity that draws very sharp distinctions between "worldly" thought and practice and the way of "holy living" to which Christians are called.

The truth of the matter, of course, is that for this way of viewing things we can appeal to the Bible for support. There is no ignoring the stark portrayal of the unredeemed life in Jeremiah 17:9, in the language of King James: "the heart is deceitful above all things and desperately wicked." Nor can we simply dismiss as an overstatement the apostolic injunction: "Do not love the world or the things in the world. The love of the Father is not in those who love the world; for all that is in the world — the desire of the flesh, the desire of the eyes, the pride in riches — comes not from the Father but from the world" (1 John 2:15-16).

Those are examples of the Bible's affirmation of the antithesis. The differences between redeemed and unredeemed consciousness are a reality that cannot be denied, and for that reason Kuyper strongly emphasized it. But he could not allow it to be the only word — or certainly the last word — about the status of fallen humanity. He knew that it was one thing to affirm the reality of the antithesis, and another thing simply to reject all that issues forth from the lives of sinful people.

Kuyper was honest enough about himself to know that the antithesis was still a presence in his own inner being. The same apostle who warns against "all that is in the world" also tells us that "what we will be has not yet been revealed" — that will only be clear to us when "he is revealed [and] we will be like him" (1 John 3:2). Sin still affects the way we think and act. And just as we are not as holy as we might be, so the unbelieving world is not always as bad as we might predict on the basis of our theology of depravity. It is a fact of our Christian experience that the church often disappoints us, while the unbelieving world sometime pleasantly surprises us. TRUE, SADLY.

So, while Kuyper continued to teach the antithesis, he also recognized the need to hold it in tension with a theological concept that allowed for the positive contributions of unregenerate humankind: *common grace.*

God's "Excellent Gifts"

---⊗⊗⊗---

The Protestant Reformers of the sixteenth century did not only argue strenuously with the Catholics; they also passionately challenged each other on theological topics. Some of the most acrimonious debates took place between the Calvinists and the Anabaptists. I have spent some time studying these debates,[1] and it seems clear to me that the reason why John Calvin found the Anabaptists of his day so frustrating was because they criticized him at points where he felt quite vulnerable.

Calvin's vulnerability was especially obvious on the subject of the effects of the Fall. He thought he had made a strong case for the idea of total depravity in critiquing what he saw as Catholicism's more optimistic view of the human condition. But the Anabaptists criticized him on precisely this point, arguing that his views about human sin were inconsistent. The

---

1. The most detailed study of these debates is Willem Balke's fine book, *Calvin and the Anabaptist Radicals,* trans. William Heynen (Grand Rapids: Eerdmans, 1981).

CONTAIN SOME TRUTH BUT STILL NOT QUITE

Anabaptists were so convinced that the unbelieving world was thoroughly corrupt that they insisted on an alternative communal lifestyle that required a clear separation from sinful culture — a pattern that we can still see today in some of their heirs among the Old Mennonites, Amish, and Hutterites. Calvin, on the other hand, regularly modified his stark depiction of human depravity by saying positive things about "worldly" thinkers and rulers. So when the Anabaptists accused him of inconsistency, he tended to bristle.

Of course, as we Calvinists are fond of pointing out, *total* depravity is not the same as *absolute* depravity. If you hold that we human beings in our fallenness are absolutely depraved, you will assume that nothing good can come forth from the sinful heart and mind. Total depravity, on the other hand, is the view that sin affects us in our totality — no part of our human nature is immune to the ravages of sin. This means that we can expect sin to show up not only in our very personal lives, but also in politics, economics, the arts, family life — in all aspects of human interaction.

That is obviously what Calvin understood by his total depravity teaching. It did not mean for him that there were not things to appreciate, and learn from, in the human community beyond the borders of the church.

"A Peculiar Grace"

Calvin's academic training had been in legal studies, and he knew that he had learned some good things from ancient pagan thinkers such as Cicero and Seneca. When we come across such people saying things that are obviously true and good, says Calvin, we should "let that admirable light of truth

[65]

shining in them teach us that the mind of man, though fallen and perverted from its wholeness, is nevertheless clothed and ornamented with God's excellent gifts." Indeed, he continues, we should accept the truth wherever we find it, and not "despise it where it shall appear, unless we wish to dishonor the Spirit of God."[2] He even at one point describes these pagan thinkers as beneficiaries of a "peculiar grace of God."[3]

Again, we have to see these comments from Calvin in relation to his harsher expressions about "the natural mind" — as we saw earlier, he did after all insist that whatever good we might see coming from such quarters is "so sullied that before God they lose all favor," and must therefore be "considered worthless."

It is tempting to see Calvin as talking out of two sides of his mouth on such matters. And in fact the seeming contradiction led one of his recent biographers simply to posit the existence of "two Calvins, coexisting uncomfortably within the same historical personage" — one a defender of "static orthodoxy" who "craved desperately for intelligibility, order, certainty," and the other "a rhetorician and a humanist" who "was inclined to celebrate the paradoxes and mystery at the heart of existence."[4]

The more generous assessment, though, is to say that Calvin thought the two could be integrated into a single coherent perspective, even though he tended to express each of them in exaggerated terms that made that integration difficult.

However that may be, Abraham Kuyper experienced the

2. Calvin, *Institutes,* II: 2, 15, 273-25.
3. Calvin, *Institutes,* II, 2, 14, 273.
4. William Bouwsma, *John Calvin: A Sixteenth-Century Portrait* (New York: Oxford University Press, 1988), 230-31.

same tension in understanding the merits and demerits of the unredeemed. And he took a step beyond Calvin in spelling out a theological perspective that made sense of his positive assessment while not sacrificing the force of his affirmation of the antithesis.

Preserving Culture

We already noticed that when John Calvin said positive things about some of the ideas that pagan thinkers came up with, he suggested that they were benefiting from a "peculiar grace of God." Kuyper not only picked up on this use of the idea of grace, he developed a whole theological perspective for using it. While the deep differences associated with the antithesis are very real in principle, he argued, they are not always obvious in reality. We often experience positive contributions from unredeemed humanity. This is due, as he saw things, to the workings of "common grace," an attitude of favor that God has toward the whole human race.

To call it "grace" is not to say that it brings salvation. Grace, for Calvin, is simply undeserved favor. Those whom God saves are not worthy of the gift of redemption through Christ. And, says Kuyper, God has some non-saving gifts that he also bestows upon the unredeemed, even though they are just as undeserving of those blessings as the redeemed are of their salvation.

The theology of common grace is a big topic — I wrote a whole book on the subject,[5] and even then I know that I did

5. Richard J. Mouw, *He Shines in All That's Fair: Culture and Common Grace* (Grand Rapids: Eerdmans, 2001).

not do the subject full justice. Part of what Kuyper meant by common grace has to do with the kind of natural blessings that visit the redeemed and the unredeemed alike — the "common" gifts that come when the Lord — to use Christ's own examples — "makes his sun rise on the evil and on the good, and sends rain on the righteous and on the unrighteous" (Matthew 5:45). It also includes God's restraining of sin: just as a leash keeps an untamed dog from doing all the harm it might otherwise cause, so God curbs evil impulses so that sinful humankind does not bring itself to a premature ruin.

But there is more to common grace for Kuyper, and it has to do with something we have already dealt with at some length: God desires to see cultural development move forward in the creation, even under sinful conditions. So God mysteriously works in positive ways in sinful humankind. This is how we are to understand the works of beauty that might be produced by a promiscuous, blaspheming artist, or the acts of justice committed by a person who speaks disdainfully about religious allegiances. Common grace is at work wherever knowledge is advancing and the arts are flourishing, as well as, in Kuyper's own words, "wherever civic virtue, a sense of domesticity, natural love, the practice of human virtue, the improvement of the public conscience, integrity, mutual loyalty among people, and a feeling for piety leaven life."[6]

The common grace that in Kuyper's system makes this possible is different from what is sometimes called *prevenient grace* — a teaching developed in some theological perspectives, especially Catholicism — to modify what might otherwise be a rather dismal view of the moral and intellectual ca-

6. Kuyper, "Common Grace," 181.

pacities of fallen human nature. On this view, God partially restored humankind's ability to think and act rightly, as a kind of "class action," so that humans in general are not quite in the desperate shape that sin might otherwise have left them in.

Kuyper was not willing to concede that much in the direction of a "natural knowledge." He saw the appeal to prevenient grace as a way of downplaying the extent of human depravity by positing a kind of automatic universal upgrade of those dimensions of human nature that have been corrupted by sin. To put it much too simply, the goal of prevenient grace *is* the upgrade; it is to raise the deeply wounded human capacities to a level where some measure of freedom to choose or reject obedience to God is made possible.

Common grace, in contrast, is in Kuyper's system God's way of bringing the cultural designs of the creation to completion. Common grace operates mysteriously in the life of, say, a self-serving government official or an unbelieving artist to harness their created talents in order to prepare the creation for the full coming of the Kingdom. In this sense, each instance of common grace — unlike the general pattern of prevenient grace — is a specifically directed move by a sovereign God to promote goals to which he is committed.

The Tension

Back in the 1970s, I was involved in an ongoing Calvinist-Mennonite dialogue. It was an exciting time for me. I spoke on a number Mennonite campuses and regularly engaged in friendly exchanges with leading Mennonite scholars about issues of peacemaking, warfare, concern for the poor, and economic systems and practices. As we pursued our differences on these matters, we often came to the conclusion that the underlying issues really had to do with different ways of understanding how we as Christians ought to evaluate and relate to the larger culture — the "world" beyond the borders of the Christian community.

On one occasion, my dialogue partner in a public setting was John Howard Yoder, one of the best-known Mennonite scholars, who influenced many non-Mennonites (including me on some important subjects) in their thinking about what it means to follow the Way of Jesus. We each made a presentation, and then we quizzed each other. After some back-and-forth between us, the moderator asked for questions from the audience. A young man stood up. "I would like it if each of you would answer this question," he said. "Where do you *really* disagree? What is the *basic* difference — when you get right down to it — between your two positions?" Professor Yoder answered first, and once he gave his answer I could do nothing to improve upon it. Here is what Yoder said: "Mouw wants to say, 'Fallen, but *created*,' and I want to say, 'Created, but *fallen.*'"

That is a great way of pointing to a fundamental issue for the way we shape our paths of discipleship. And Yoder had the two "sides" right. He did a good job of capturing a key theme in my Kuyperian perspective: the cultures in which we find ourselves in this sinful world are indeed fallen — but they still reflect the original creation. To repeat what I quoted earlier from H. Richard Niebuhr: The cultural world in which we presently live "is perverted good, not evil . . . it is evil as perversion and not as badness of being."

Avoiding the Twin Dangers

I said earlier that, in contrast to Calvin, Kuyper integrated the positive and negative aspects of fallen humanity into a single perspective. Of course, the integration is not a very neat one. The antithesis and common grace still stand in tension. But by offering a theological analysis of each of them, Kuyper did at least place them into a larger theological perspective. And for him they functioned primarily as tools for explaining what actually goes on in the world. When an obviously wicked person does some unexpectedly good thing, we Kuyperians can say, "That's common grace at work." When a sinner acts according to the total depravity script, or when we feel the continuing pull of sin in our own lives, we can take this as confirmation that the antithesis is real.

I once heard a political scientist in Amsterdam, an expert on Kuyper's political career, say that Kuyper made highly effective use of the two themes as a practicing parliamentary leader. When Kuyper saw the need to forge an alliance with some other party on a specific issue, he would explain the temporary alliance to his Calvinist followers in terms of common grace. When he insisted on taking a stand that none of the leaders of other parties would support him in, he preached the antithesis.

Generally speaking, Kuyper seemed to do a good job of holding the two ideas in a creative tension. This has not always been the case, though, among his followers. Some have so strongly emphasized the antithesis that they have been given to a rather consistent pattern of "over-against-ness." Others have been too quick to assume the workings of common grace, thereby running the risk of binding themselves to people and things that tempt us to disobedience.

How can we avoid the real dangers in either direction? If we are going to use Kuyper's ideas about these matters for our own time, that is a crucial question. To address it, we need to think more broadly about the workability and relevance of Kuyper's overall perspective for the changing cultural context in which we find ourselves in the twenty-first century.

Kuyper for the Twenty-First Century

Kuyperian Aggiornamento

―――∞∞∞――――

The Catholic Church's Vatican II — the Second Vatican Council — lasted for a little over three years, from 1962 to 1965, and brought about some major changes in Catholic thought and practice. The Catholics describe this time of renewal using a wonderful Italian word: *aggiornamento* (pronounced "ah-jawr-na-men-to"); it means "updating."

At a few points in my explanation thus far of some key themes in Kuyper's thought, I have been tempted to start doing some significant Kuyperian *aggiornamento*. But I have for the most part resisted that temptation in order to lay out his overall theological perspective on culture more or less in the terms that he intended. Now in this chapter, and a few that follow, I will engage in some *aggiornamento* — some necessary updating — regarding some elements in Kuyper's system that need fixing for our present-day Christian cultural calling. Kuyper was very much a person of his day. This means that on some subjects he had views that were seriously misguided. That is certainly true, as we will see, of his racial views. On some other subjects he was, at the very least, intemperate, given to rhetorical excesses when dealing with other positions. But he was also profoundly insightful about many important issues — so insightful that it is well worth the effort of engaging in some Kuyperian *aggiornamento*.

Learning from Bavinck

Kuyper's excessive rhetoric leaps out at me, for example, when I see how, in his Stone Lectures, he compares Calvinism to other Christian traditions. He is especially fond of telling us how his kind of Calvinist theology is far superior to both Catholic and Anabaptist thought — he even slips in a dig or two at the Lutherans!

I want to push the Kuyperian project in a different direction, an ecumenical one. That word "ecumenical" isn't a very popular one in many circles today, but it is a fine word. It comes from the Greek word *oikomene,* which means "the household." To be ecumenical in the best sense is to be aware of the whole Christian household.

Actually, Kuyper had a good ecumenical model available to him in a person that was very close to him: his younger colleague, Herman Bavinck. Another brilliant thinker, Bavinck worked closely with Kuyper to develop views that are associated with "neo-Calvinism." Bavinck differed from Kuyper, however, in two important respects. One is that he stuck with a carefully pursued scholarly agenda. Kuyper was a public theologian without peer who engaged in theological reflection on the run as the leader of a political party, a founder of a denomination, a newspaper editorialist, and in other roles as well. Bavinck, on the other hand, worked almost exclusively in an academic setting, first at a theological school in Kampen, and then at Amsterdam's Free University.

The second difference, though, is more substantial. Bavinck's tone was more moderate, and he treated views with which he disagreed with much charity — unlike Kuyper, who often came across as a polemicist. Bavinck's kinder and gentler orthodoxy holds out much promise for us in North America, especially since his works are being assigned these days to students in a variety of seminaries on the more conservative end of the Reformed and Presbyterian communities.

Take Bavinck's comments about Islam. In one of his hefty volumes in systematic theology he writes that "in the past the [Christian] study of religions was pursued exclusively in the interest of dogmatics and apologetics." This meant, he says, that Mohammed and others "were simply considered imposters, enemies of God, accomplices of the devil." Now that their perspectives are becoming "more precisely known," however, "this interpretation has proven to be untenable." We do well to search for the ways, he insists, in which such perspectives display "an illumination by the Logos, a working of God's Spirit."[1]

Bavinck showed a similar appreciation for the views of those within the Christian tradition that Calvinists had often treated with pure hostility. Here he is offering advice on how we ought to assess the emphasis on "good works" in Catholic thought and practice:

[W]e must remind ourselves that the Catholic righteousness by good works is vastly preferable to a protestant

---

1. Herman Bavinck, *Reformed Dogmatics*, Vol. 1: *Prologomena*, trans. John Vriend (Grand Rapids: Baker Academic, 2003), 318.

righteousness by good doctrine. At least righteousness by good works benefits one's neighbor, whereas righteousness by good doctrine only produces lovelessness and pride. Furthermore, we must not blind ourselves to the tremendous faith, genuine repentance, complete surrender and the fervent love for God and neighbor evident in the lives and work of many Catholic Christians. The Christian life is so rich that it develops its full glory not just in a single form or within the walls of one church.[2]

I often wonder what Kuyper thought of this kind of thing, coming from his close colleague and friend. My own sense is that it is important for us today to keep a healthy dose of Bavinck in the Kuyperian mix.

Gifts from Others

There is a part of me, of course, that lifts up cheers for Kuyper's strong Calvinism. His theology on the issues of depravity, election, covenant, and the like is mine as well.

If you push me hard, I will say that the best way to understand and explain Kuyper's theology of culture is to be explicit about its connection to all that good Reformed theological content. I do, however, see ways in which it can connect effectively with other theological/confessional traditions.

And I really do want to see those connections made. I know that Calvinism is not the only way of thinking clearly

2. Herman Bavinck, *The Certainty of Faith*, trans. Harry der Nederlanden (Toronto: Paidea Press, 1980), 27.

about the Christian faith. I heartily endorse Bavinck's comment, quoted above, that the "Christian life is so rich that it develops its full glory not just in a single form or within the walls of one church." So I am interested in further developing Kuyper's insights about culture in conversation with other Christian traditions — and, equally important, as we will see in the next chapter, with Christians from diverse cultural contexts.

And that has to be genuine dialogue, in which the insights move in both directions. I have learned enough from other Christian traditions to know that a dialogue with others about Kuyperian themes will end up enriching Kuyperianism. Such conversation can help us draw on the riches of other traditions as a way of allowing Kuyper's theology itself to "develop its full glory."

Race: Adding Another "Neo"

‑‑‑‑‑‑‑‑∞‑‑‑‑‑‑‑‑

We have already seen that Kuyper was not an uncritical follower of John Calvin. He had some serious disagreements with the sixteenth-century Reformer, especially on questions about how Christians should think about, and behave in, the public arena. The fact of these differences with Calvin is what led to the labeling of Kuyper's way of thinking as "neo-Calvinism." And it is important to take that same "neo" label and apply it to "Kuyperian" itself as we think today about the application of Kuyper's thought to contemporary life.

Vincent Bacote, a professor at Wheaton College, has made this case nicely for attaching the "neo" prefix by way of reworking some of Kuyper's thoughts. "To be Kuyperian today," he writes, "we must understand the challenges of our era (hopefully with even half the prescience Kuyper had about the future) and develop theologically grounded approaches to public engagement." This means, says Bacote, that we must work out a *neo-Kuyperian* approach.[1]

1. Vincent Bacote, *The Spirit in Public Theology: Appropriating the Legacy of Abraham Kuyper* (Grand Rapids: Baker Academic, 2005).

"Not for Whites Only"

Bacote has a very good reason for making it clear that he is a neo-Kuyperian. An African American evangelical, he once gave a very insightful lecture at a conference, to which he gave the title, "Not for Whites Only: The Multi-cultural Relevance of Neo-Calvinism." In that lecture he confronted head-on the racist elements in Kuyper's thought. We need to hold on to the good ideas in Kuyper, Bacote argued, while at the same time doing a "neo" job on some bad ones. And on the subject of race, there are some bad ideas indeed in Kuyper's thought.

The topic of race is one about which we need to do more than just a little *aggiornamento*. Much of Kuyper's thinking on this subject requires straightforward repudiation. This is especially important to be clear about, since there are some whose knowledge of Kuyper is limited to his reputation as one of the influences on Afrikaner *apartheid* thinking that long characterized white Dutch Reformed culture in South Africa.

Kuyper never visited South Africa; his interest in South Africa grew mainly out of his political support for the struggle of the Dutch Reformed *Boers* against British rule in South Africa. But he was known to set forth views on occasion about the place of the African continent in general in the larger picture of global cultural diversity.

In his 1898 Princeton lectures, for example, Kuyper wrote about African culture that "[n]o impulse for any higher life has ever gone forth" from that part of the world.[2] This, along with many other things he said on the subject of race, made it clear that he considered persons of African descent to be inferior. Indeed, he even suggests that the best thing that can hap-

2. Kuyper, *Lectures*, 35.

pen to blacks is interracial marriage — which, he said, would help them to gain some of the benefits of white blood. Just as the quality of plant life can be improved, Kuyper argued, by "the crossing of different breeds," so "the commingling of blood" can be a strategy of cultural progress in Africa.[3]

Of course, in saying that kind of thing, Kuyper was walking a different path than those who would use some of his ideas to promote the separation *(apartheid)* of the races — *apartheid* policy forbade intermarriage. But he was still in his own way clearly reinforcing the idea of the inferiority of black Africans.

"Black Kuyperianism"

Like Bacote, though, some black Christian leaders in South Africa did not let this kind of thing deter them from mining Kuyper's thought for positive themes to be employed in their own struggles. The black Reformed theologian Russel Botman provides us with a good case in point in this regard. He notes that "Kuyper has had [both] an oppressive influence and also a liberative influence on South Africa."[4] While "Afrikaner-Dutch Kuyperianism had used the negative aspects of Kuyper," Botman observes, "it was the task of Black Kuyperianism to select the positive aspects and present their theological relevance to South Africa."[5] In this regard, Botman cites the example of another black theologian, Allan

3. Kuyper, *Lectures,* 35-36.
4. H. Russel Botman, "Is Blood Thicker than Justice? The Legacy of Abraham Kuyper for Southern Africa," in Luis Lugo, *Religion, Pluralism, and Public Life: Abraham Kuyper's Legacy for the Twenty-First Century* (Grand Rapids: Eerdmans, 2000), 343.
5. Botman, "Is Blood Thicker than Justice?" 344.

Boesak, who appealed to Kuyper in support of the struggle for racial justice:

> We believe passionately with Abraham Kuyper that there is not a single inch of life that does not fall under the lordship of Christ. . . . Here the Reformed tradition comes so close to the African idea of the wholeness of life that these two should combine to renew the thrust that was brought to Christian life by the followers of Calvin.[6]

Thus, says Botman, we must simply acknowledge that "[t]he real Kuyper was both these things: a praiseworthy Reformed theologian who, regrettably, held to the potentially oppressive core value of separateness."[7]

That is a generous assessment — but also an encouraging one for those of us who are working on a "neo-Kuyperianism."

Thinking Cross-Culturally

Boesak's observation that Kuyper's broad sense of Christ's Lordship "comes so close to the African idea of the wholeness of life" points us to another underdeveloped subject in Kuyper's thought: the ways in which our understanding of the gospel can be enriched by paying careful attention to the many different cultural contexts that have come to characterize God's creation. This is a large subject, and it needs much attention. The ongoing discussion of "Christ and culture" has

6. Allan Boesak, *Black and Reformed: Apartheid, Liberation, and the Calvinist Tradition* (New York: Orbis Press, 1984), 87; quoted by Botman, "Is Blood Thicker than Justice?" 344.

7. Botman, "Is Blood Thicker than Justice?" 354.

to expand to tackle the important contemporary agenda of "Christ and *the cultures.*"

Here again, Herman Bavinck points Kuyperians in a fruitful direction. In his discussion of the idea of the image of God,[8] Bavinck observed that the creation of humans in the divine image in the Genesis creation narrative "is not the end but the beginning of God's journey with mankind." In mandating that the first human pair be "fruitful and multiply," God was making it clear that "[n]ot the man alone, nor the man and the woman together, but only the whole of humanity together is the fully developed image of God," for "[t]he image of God is much too rich for it to be fully realized in a single human being, however richly gifted that human being may be."

Bavinck goes on to insist that this collective sense of the divine image in human beings "is not a static entity but extends and unfolds itself" in the rich diversity of humankind spread over many places and times. We will finally see this image in its fullness, he says, when the redeemed will be gathered into the New Jerusalem from many tribes and tongues and peoples to "bring into [the City] the glory and the honor of the nations" (Revelation 21:26). This reference to "the glory and the honor" that will be received into the City in the end-time certainly refers to the redeemed *peoples* who will be gathered into the City from many tribes and nations. But Kuyper and Bavinck were also convinced that it also referred to the *works* of many cultures — with those diverse redeemed peoples bearing the cultural achievements of human history as tributes to the Lord of creation.

As Kuyper put it in commenting on the New Jerusalem vi-

---

8. Herman Bavinck, *Reformed Dogmatics,* Vol. 2: *God and Creation,* trans. John Vriend (Grand Rapids: Baker Academic, 2004), 577-78.

sion at the end of the Book of Revelation, in that City "[t]he whole reborn humanity stands before God as a holy unity that is athrob with life," and this fully redeemed humanity "does not remain on its knees in uninterrrupted worship of God," instead engaging in "new callings, new life-tasks, new commissions." The life of the future age *"will be a full human life* which will exhibit all the glory that God in the first creation had purposed and appointed for the same, but which by us was sinned away."[9]

This theme deserves considerable theological development. Indeed that development is an important preparation for a celebration that will take place before the divine throne someday, as described also in the Bible's vision of the end-time:

> After this I looked, and there was a great multitude that no one could count, from every nation, from all tribes and peoples and languages, standing before the throne and before the Lamb, robed in white, with palm branches in their hands. They cried out in a loud voice, saying, "Salvation belongs to our God who is seated on the throne, and to the Lamb!" (Revelation 7:9-10)

9. Abraham Kuyper, *The Revelation of St. John,* trans. John Hendrik DeVries (Grand Rapids: William B. Eerdmans Publishing Co., 1935), 331-32.

Kuyper for Evangelicals

———— ∞∞∞ ————

M y conviction that Kuyper's theology of culture can be
attractive to people who do not necessarily share his
Calvinist convictions on issues like predestination and the
Reformed/Presbyterian theology of church and sacraments
has a basis in my actual experience. I regularly teach a "Perspectives on Culture" course at Fuller Seminary, and I devote
some class time to discussing Kuyper's views. There are typically more than a hundred students in the class, and they
come from a wide variety of denominations and non-
denominational churches. Usually the Calvinists are a small
minority.

What those students have in common is their evangelical
identity. They may be Baptists or Anglicans or Presbyterians
or Pentecostals or Wesleyans or "independents" or whatever
— we have students from over one hundred denominations.
But what they bring to those other churchly and theological
identities is a profound commitment to the New Testament
teaching that we are lost sinners who need to look to the aton-
ing work of Christ on Calvary as our only hope for salvation.

The enthusiastic embrace of that message is at the heart of evangelicalism.

The problem with a lot of evangelicalism, though, is that it often focuses exclusively on personal religion. True: Jesus is a personal Savior who wants us to have a personal relationship with him. But that is not all Jesus is. And for evangelicals who want a solid theological basis for the "more" of Jesus' redemptive work, it is often very exciting to learn about an important Christian thinker, one who himself experienced the transforming power of the gospel in his own personal life, who also insisted that "there is not a square inch in the whole domain of our human existence over which Christ, who is sovereign over all, does not cry 'Mine!'"

We can think of Kuyper as an important theologian of the rule of Christ. Jesus is a Savior, but also a King. Christ's Kingship is a theme that shows up — at least as formal acknowledgement — in just about every Christian theological system. Kuyper's theology took it seriously as something that had to be worked out in considerable detail for our understanding of the calling of the Christian community in God's world — a world that extends well beyond the boundaries of the church. That is a good reason for promoting the cause of a more "ecumenical" Kuyper.

Being "Spirit-Filled"

I won't get into a lot of specifics about how various traditions can tap into Kuyper's thinking about culture. But I will offer one substantive example here.

Al Wolters has reflected on the ways in which many of Kuyper's recent followers have been so condemning of a pietistic anti-intellectualism that they have failed to follow Kuyper's own example in grounding cultural discipleship in a vital spirituality. This is a serious problem, Wolters insists, and he points us to resources that can provide new spiritual fiber for present-day neo-Calvinists. In addition to Catholic and Eastern Orthodox practices of spirituality, he sees the charismatic renewal as offering some help. Neo-Calvinism, Wolters observes, can benefit greatly from "[t]he power, vitality and emotional spontaneity of the charismatic movement, as well as its openness to the charismatic gifts, its emphasis on the effectiveness of prayer, and its acknowledgement of the reality of the demonic."[1]

I am happy to say that I spend a lot of time with people who have been shaped by Pentecostal/charismatic teachings. They have had a good influence on my theology and my understanding of the spiritual life. I have often worried about the fact that there are aspects of the ministry of the Holy Spirit that have not received sufficient attention in my kind of Reformed theology.

Kuyper clearly sensed that defect. He wrote a fairly large volume on the Holy Spirit, and he said many things that my Pentecostal and charismatic friends would find pleasing. But he also said some things that would prod them a bit in their theology. Here, for example, is what I consider to be a profound theological comment: "the work of the Holy Spirit," Kuyper writes, "consists in leading all creation *to its destiny,* the final purpose of which is the glory of God."[2] Geerhardus Vos, a friend of Kuyper who represented Kuyper's perspective

---

1. Al Wolters, "What is to Be Done . . . toward a Neocalvinist Agenda?" October 14, 2005. http://www.cardus.ca/comment/article/282/.

2. Abraham Kuyper, *The Work of the Holy Spirit,* trans. Henri DeVries (New York: Funk and Wagnalls, 1900), 22.

as a distinguished professor at Princeton Seminary for many years, emphasized the same thing, arguing that the primary focus of the Holy Spirit's ministry is to prepare the whole creation for God's glorious future.[3] And this future will display the gathering in of the works of culture into the eternal Kingdom. To be sure, the products and processes of human culture throughout history need to be cleansed and purified in order properly to glorify God. But, for Kuyper and Vos, this is an important aspect of the sanctifying work of the Spirit. These works too will be purged of impurities in order to be received into the Kingdom. The fire that appeared at Pentecost as individual "tongues of fire" will in the end-time become the refiner's fire described by the Apostle Peter, when he foretells that in "the coming of the day of God" all of creation "will be set ablaze and dissolved" to prepare "for new heavens and a new earth, where righteousness is at home" (2 Peter 3:12-13).

Pentecostal and charismatic theologies have provided us with profound insights into the transforming power of the Spirit in our individual lives, as well as in the community of believers. Kuyper's theology can be seen as building on that emphasis. He emphasizes that what happens to us in our individual lives and in the fellowship of Spirit-filled believers is part of the Spirit's larger work of "making new" the whole creation.

3. Geerhardus Vos, "The Eschatological Aspect of the Pauline Conception of the Spirit," in *Biblical and Theological Studies,* by the Faculty of Princeton Theological Seminary (New York: Charles Scribner's Sons, 1912), 209-59.

World-Viewing

⸺ ∞ ⸺

I mentioned earlier that "world and life view" was one of Kuyper's favorite phrases. Those of us who have been influenced by him have regularly shortened the phrase a little, preferring to talk about the need for a "worldview." This focus on worldview has been our way of following Kuyper's lead in insisting that our cultural involvements, including our scholarly pursuits, have to be consciously guided by our understanding of our place in the larger scheme of things.

Brian Walsh and Richard Middleton, in a book they wrote from a Kuyperian perspective, offered a concise way of understanding what goes into having a worldview. A person's worldview, they said, answers these four questions: Who am I? Where am I? What's wrong? What is the remedy?[1]

Even though those questions are put in a simple form, they get at very big issues. What is the nature of the human person? How do we as humans fit into the larger scheme of things? What, in the most basic sense, is the fundamental defect in our

1. Brian J. Walsh and J. Richard Middleton, *The Transforming Vision: Shaping a Christian World View* (Downers Grove: Intervarsity Press, 1984), 35.

condition that gives rise to so many problems and so much suffering? And what would it take to correct that basic defect?

Our answers to those questions really do make a big difference in how we live and think. Our understanding of human createdness and sinfulness stands in stark contrast to assumptions about human nature set forth by, say, Freudians, New Agers, and Nietzschean nihilists. And to see ourselves as part of a larger reality fashioned by a holy God suggests a distinction between Creator and creation that rules out not only a thoroughgoing naturalism, but also the various animisms and the all-species-are-equal views of neo-paganism. The biblical perspective on salvation and the afterlife differs significantly from conceptions of human flourishing that are taken for granted in various ethical and therapeutic schemes.

It is clear also that our Christian answers to those questions differ from those given by other religious perspectives on life. For example, I once served on an interreligious panel where my Buddhist counterpart described what she saw as her basic difference with me very succinctly: on the Christian view, she said, we are all sinners in need of redemption, while in her Buddhist perspective we are presently ignorant people who need enlightenment. That is a basic worldview difference, and it has implications across the board for how we will deal with a variety of intellectual, spiritual, political, and moral questions. Kuyper would have appreciated her clarity on the basic issue of worldview!

Beholding

The Catholic philosopher Josef Pieper was once invited by a sculptor friend to give some talks in her studio to a group of her fellow artists. In one of his talks he told the artists that the early Greek philosopher Anaxagoras wrote something like a catechism for his students. One of the questions posed by Anaxagoras was, "Why are you here on earth?" to which he gave the simple reply, "To behold." Pieper applied this comment of Anaxagoras to the artistic task, but it also works well for understanding the Christian life as such. God wants us to engage in beholding, in a special kind of "seeing." As Pieper put it to his artist audience, we have to look carefully at people and things, directing our gaze to more than "the tangible surface of reality." Here Pieper used a Latin phrase from the ancient mystics: *ubi amor, ibi oculus* — roughly, "where there is love, there is seeing."[2]

This is really what Kuyper was getting at with the idea of worldview. When our lives have been transformed by God's grace, we see many things in new ways. And this seeing is guided by love, by an abiding desire to care about what God cares about — to rejoice in what makes God's heart glad and to grieve about what saddens him. That kind of seeing, "beholding," has profound implications for how we view people and ideas and the products and processes of culture.

On the Move

I am grateful for the influence this worldview perspective has had for my own spiritual and intellectual journey. But I have to admit that some of the talk about worldview makes me a little nervous these days. When I hear folks insist on the need

2. Josef Pieper, *Only the Lover Sings: Art and Contemplation,* trans. Luther Krait (San Francisco: Ignatius Press, 1990), 72-74.

for all of us to "have" a Christian worldview, I worry about the static picture that evokes. It suggests that a worldview is something that we can possess, a thing that we can "own" or just "get." That in turn gives the impression, I fear, that having a worldview means that we are equipped with a set of answers, or the capacity to generate those answers fairly easily, when we encounter important questions. I don't like the "packaged" feel of all that.

I am more inclined these days to think not so much about *having a worldview,* but rather about *engaging in world-viewing.* That has a more dynamic feel. Our "beholding" must be an active process. It is something we do on a journey. One of my favorite verses in this regard is Psalm 119:105: "Your word is a lamp to my feet and a light to my path." Being a Christian worldviewer means allowing the Bible to shed light on the paths we walk.

I struggle as a Christian with topics that are beyond anything Kuyper ever thought about. Questions about responding to terrorism, the proper use of new information technologies in higher education, the implications of new brain research discoveries for our understanding of the human soul — tough questions in our challenging new world. There is very little in these subjects about which I can confidently speak of "*the* Christian perspective." But that does not mean that I may give up on the struggle, left to act off the cuff. I have to keep at the task of worldviewing, of shining the light of God's Word on the new realities that I encounter along the way.

My commitment to worldviewing certainly means that I will insist on asking certain kinds of questions. Take stem cell research. When someone wants my verdict on the use of "stored" frozen human embryos — which have a limited "shelf life" — for important diabetes research, I cannot avoid asking about the relevance to this complex topic of what the psalmist says about his pre-natal relationship to God: "For it was you who formed my inward parts; you knit me together in my mother's womb" (Psalm 139:13). Or the much-debated issues today about divorce or same-sex attraction. Whatever I might be inclined to accept from "expert opinion" or my own experience, I cannot avoid the question: "But what does the Bible mean to teach us about such matters?"

Josef Pieper's Latin phrase again: *ubi amor, ibi oculus* — "where there is love, there is seeing." And God has lovingly provided his Word for us as we travel, so that when its light shines on our path, we see things we would have otherwise missed.

Will the Bell Still Toll?

The Christian people who were Kuyper's closest support-
ers in his day had a slogan that they used in describing
him: "the bell-ringer for the common people." Kuyper had a
special affection for the "little people" of Dutch society, peasant farmers and urban laborers. But that affection extended
to leaders in various cultural spheres: civic leaders, artists,
business owners, and journalists.

While the term was not one that he used, Kuyper was an
advocate for "the theology of the laity." People who have
worked on that kind of theology have rightly insisted that
laypeople — those who are not ordained for "clergy" activities
— have their own ministries. And this is not limited to help-
ing pastors in their church work. That should happen, of
course; laypeople have their own important role in the activities of the local congregation. But what we do outside of the
church must also be seen as ministry.

Kuyper wanted the church to be, among other things, a
sending-out station. Obviously we have to be careful here. The
primary reason to go to church is to worship God. The Lord

wants us to gather as his people in order to acknowledge that he alone is worthy of our worship. Gathering in the presence of God for the purpose of praise and adoration — this is an essential feature of worship.

But to worship God is to acknowledge his Kingship and Lordship. It is to bow in the presence of his authority. And this should have implications for how we see our daily lives. When we leave church each Sunday, we should have marching orders for service in the Kingdom. That is a great vision of what the church must do and be — for the "common people," those who come from a busy world of work and play to gather in the presence of their true and righteous Sovereign.

How we can be sure the kind of bell that Kuyper liked to ring keeps ringing today?

A Larger Kingdom

When I hear people equate "church" and "Kingdom" I inwardly (and sometimes visibly) cringe. You don't have to go into a church to do something related to the Kingdom. What we need to be reminded of in church is that the world in which we live out our daily interactions — at work, on the tennis court, in our family lives, entering voting booths, sitting in front of television sets — all that *is* the Kingdom.

To be sure, the church is *also* a Kingdom place. Christ also rules there — and in a special way. In that worshiping space we encounter through our worship the King who sends us every week, when we leave the four walls of the church building, into his larger Kingdom.

Jesus in an Insurance Office

A friend of mine who owned an insurance agency was very clear about all of this. In college he had learned about Kuyper's views, and he saw himself as doing exactly what Kuyper called for. He gave me an example of what this meant for him that captured the message for me in a marvelous way.

He was asked to serve on a panel of Christian leaders, to share how they apply their faith to their daily work. The other three talked primarily about personal qualities, such as honesty, as well as the need to look for opportunities to witness to others about Christ. The leader who spoke just before my friend did testified that he instructed his secretary to set aside one noon hour a week where this person could be alone in his office for prayer and Bible study. "I need to get away from the hustle and bustle of business," he said, "to spend some time with my Lord."

My friend went last. He began his own comments by affirming what the previous person had reported. "Yes, I do that too," he said. "I want to spend some quiet time in my office, alone with my Lord." He continued: "But I also want to sense the Lord's presence *in* the hustle and bustle of business." The week before, he said, he had met with a newly married couple to talk with them about their insurance needs. "I was dealing with some of the most important questions they could be asking. How do we view the future? What do we really care about as we plan our lives together? As I talked with them about these things, I knew that my Lord was right there, watching over my shoulder as I sketched out an insurance plan for them. God cares about how I write insurance policies!"

Identifying Resource Centers

That insurance agent was looking at his daily work in exactly the way Kuyper would want him to. And he happened to learn this in an environment — the Dutch Calvinist community in North America. The Kuyperian vision in that community gripped the imagination of insurance agents, grocers, farmers, car dealers — and to some degree their sons and daughters who became lawyers, physicians, professors, and airline executives.

Today, however, we face new cultural realities: the Internet, "knowledge workers," a global economy, multiculturalism, and biotech research. The mandate is to see ourselves as being called by the Lord to promote the cause of his Kingdom on all of these square inches that for us are new territory for our walk of obedient service.

Where can we expect the bell to be rung today? What resources are necessary for equipping God's people for the every-square-inch discipleship? I'm convinced that we need to look in new ways — in ways Kuyper did not anticipate — to the local church as a place where the bell has to be rung loudly and clearly.

Enhancing the Church's Role

───⊶⊷───

Kuyper gave the church a fairly limited role in the overall picture of cultural obedience. He had good reasons for this, and some of those reasons still hold. There is, for example, at least one pragmatic reason for limiting the culture-guiding role of the institutional church, and that has to do with the actual makeup of local churches. Except in unusual situations, the people who need to be engaging in mutual encouragement and strategizing for specific areas of calling are not likely to be available in significant numbers in a particular congregation.

Vocation-Specific Strategizing

A case in point: in 1977 a group of North American Christians who were actively involved in the arts — painters, sculptors, art historians, curators, patrons — formed an organization called Christians in the Visual Arts, CIVA. The organization has flourished, sponsoring conferences, symposia, exhibits, and publications. Here is how CIVA describes its reason for being:

> It is our purpose to encourage Christians in the visual arts to develop their particular callings to the highest professional level possible; to learn how to deal with specific problems in the field without compromising our faith and our standard of artistic endeavor; to provide opportunities for sharing work and ideas; to foster intelligent understanding, a spirit of trust, and a cooperative relationship between those in the arts, the church, and society; and ultimately, to establish a Christian presence within the secular art world.[1]

That is precisely the kind of rationale that Kuyper envisioned for a group of believers who band together for faithful discipleship in a specific field of cultural activity. What has changed today is that there is little need for distinctively Calvinist or Catholic or Pentecostal or Lutheran "CIVAs." Christians are coming together from various churches to reflect on obedience to Christ in specific areas of cultural engagement — an exciting "ecumenical" project in our day!

Church Sponsorship?

Now, could this kind of thing be done under the sponsorship of a church or a group of churches? Of course, especially if the right conditions prevailed, such as a sufficient interest on the part of the church, a commitment to making it happen, and

---

1. http://www.civa.org/about.php.

the ability to provide expert guidance on the issues described in the CIVA statement.

In fact, this is already happening. Redeemer Presbyterian Church in New York City has a creative and flourishing Center for Faith and Work,[2] which includes in its various programs an Arts Ministry outreach — and Kuyperian materials are recommended readings for the people who participate in this program.

I don't see any reason why this kind of arrangement — a church-based gathering of persons who are seeking to be disciples of Christ in a specific vocational field — should be troublesome to a present-day Kuyperian. Kuyper's own objections to putting art guilds under the ecclesiastical umbrella had to do in large part with the fact that there had been a long period in Western history when the church was the primary patron of the arts. This meant that artists were very tied to "churchly" projects. Indeed, it meant that much art actually found its home within the walls of church buildings. Kuyper wanted artists to pursue their vocations in the larger cultural arena. And that was certainly a worthy motive.

In our own day, however, we have a very different problem. Churches in recent years have not always been very encouraging to artists as they pursue their vocations "out there" in the "secular" arena. Redeemer Presbyterian Church ministers in Manhattan, where there are many practitioners and devotees of the arts who often have felt a disconnect between their creative efforts and the preachments of the churches. For a major congregation not only to give its blessing to the arts as an important arena for Christian service, but actually to convene artists to wrestle with the detailed challenges they face in pur-

2. http://www.redeemer.com/connect/faith_and_work/.

suing their vocation — this (along with parallel Redeemer programs for persons in the financial services) is a wonderful outreach into the larger culture.

Seeing to It

The problems with church sponsorship of vocation-specific groups ought not to be seen, then, as matters of principle. The difficulties are basically practical ones. Most local churches do not have a significant number of artists in their membership. It is not feasible for such congregations to take on a convening ministry in this area of cultural discipleship. And the same holds for other vocation-specific groups: surgeons, nurses, Christians in the entertainment industry, airline personnel.

But that does not mean that those congregations can be excused from their obligations with regard to vocation-specific convenings. The church has an important responsibility in *seeing to it* that Christians not only understand their daily lives as Kingdom activity, but also seek out other Christians for mutual discernment in the face of the significant challenges we face in our efforts to be faithful to the gospel in the larger cultural arena.

How to exercise this churchly responsibility? We should certainly not expect preachers to function as experts on the issues people face in their specific vocations. Pastors do not need to have a grasp on the intricacies of art history or parenting or economics or the natural sciences. If sermons and ecclesiastical pronouncements are to make plain God's will on such matters, they must stay firmly grounded in what is clearly stated in the Scriptures. This means, for example, that we can boldly state that God cares deeply about the poor and oppressed, but when we offer the verdict that God typically prefers government-controlled welfare programs over initiatives originating in the private sector (or the other way around), we are taking a step away from what can be shown to be solidly grounded in the Scriptures. And the same holds for other areas of expertise.

Too often, though, recognizing all of that leads immediately to the conclusion that worshipers must leave the church service to struggle individually with the application of what they have heard for their daily decision-making. That is too quick. Between the gathered church and the individual Christian going out into the world to struggle alone with specifics, there is an important intermediate area of activity. Christians must be encouraged to form a variety of organizations that focus on specific areas of cultural involvement, in order to engage in the kind of communal reflection necessary to develop a Christian "mind" for the area in question. And it is important that this encouragement comes from the church — from the teaching ministry of the local congregation.

The church today has an obligation to issue the mandate for believers to find and participate in communal arrangements for Christian discernment regarding cultural discipleship. But it isn't just a mandate. There is also a need for people in specific vocations to know that they are being given *encouragement and support* from the worshiping community.

My own congregation, Bel Air Presbyterian Church, is located near Hollywood, and many of our members are employed in "the industry." Frequently our pastors will call attention to the importance of Christian involvement in Hollywood. Sometimes we are asked to lay hands on and pray for those who will be pursuing those callings during the coming week. That can be done in other contexts and for other vocations as well. It takes no special "expertise" to pray intelligently for our fellow Christians who face difficult challenges in their daily lives and vocations.

Nurturing Cultural Patience

⸺ ❦ ⸺

Several years ago I met in Washington, D.C., with a group of about two dozen young Christian professionals who worked in various congressional staffs, lobby groups, federal agencies, and think tanks. I found them to be a very thoughtful group, intensely interested in integrating their basic evangelical convictions with the day-to-day pursuit of their work assignments.

As these young evangelicals talked about the theological issues that most concerned them in their work in the public arena, one of the dominant questions that occupied their minds was the degree to which can we expect success in our efforts to promote public righteousness during this time when we still await the return of Christ. In struggling with this issue they were clearly attempting to find an alternative to two options that evangelicals often have seen themselves as having to choose between. Either we try as much as possible to stay out of the cultural mainstream, standing over against it as we wait for the Final Judgment, or we must attempt to take over the culture.

We can see both options at work during the past century. The "fundamentalist-modernist" controversy of the first few decades of the twentieth century led religious conservatives to a strong sense of alienation from the Protestant mainline, as well as from the dominant patterns of the larger culture. This posture began to change around mid-century, but the changes became especially visible around 1980, when the "faithful remnant" mentality of much of evangelicalism suddenly transformed into a sense of being "the Moral Majority" — one of the better-known organizations of "the Christian Right." That kind of activism was often accused of "theocratic" motives — a desire to return the United States to what many of the evangelical activists saw as its original status as "a Christian nation."

The young evangelical professionals with whom I met were not theocrats who were hoping for a Christian takeover of the public arena. And they were certainly not world-fleeing fundamentalists. They were trying to stake out an alternative approach. Kuyper would have supported their effort. In his thinking about political life, he was convinced that there are good Christian reasons for trying to accomplish some good things, even though we know that we are not likely to achieve any major victories.

The Kuyperian motive for involvement in public life is not to win the battle for righteousness in the here-and-now. None of us is the Messiah. The world has already been given one supremely excellent Messiah, and he has guaranteed that in the final reckoning everything will be made right. In the meantime, though, we must take advantage of every opportunity available to us to do whatever we can to promote his cause — knowing all the time that the final victory will happen only when the Lord decides that it is ready to happen.

Seeking the Welfare

Kuyper's approach has clear biblical grounding. For example, there came a point in the life of ancient Israel when God's chosen people were carried off into captivity in the wicked city of Babylon. This was a troubling situation for them: no temple in which to worship the Lord, no godly rulers, no laws based on revealed guidance about how to live. Then the Lord gave the prophet Jeremiah some new instructions for the captive Israelites. He told them that God wanted them to build houses for their families to live in, and to plant crops for their livelihood. God also instructed them to "multiply there," marrying and producing children. But then he gave them this assignment for their lives as citizens: "But seek the welfare of the city where I have sent you into exile, and pray to the Lord on its behalf, for in its welfare you will find your welfare" (Jeremiah 29:5-7). The Hebrew word for "welfare" here is *shalom,* which is often translated as "peace" but also includes the notions of justice and righteousness.

Similar advice is given to the New Testament church. The Apostle Peter addresses believers who, like those ancient Israelites in Babylon, are "aliens and exiles" in the places where they live. And he gives a similar assignment: "Conduct yourselves honorably among the Gentiles," he says, "so that, though they malign you as evildoers, they may see your honorable deeds, and glorify God when he comes to judge" (1 Peter 2:11-12).

The mandate should be clear: we have to care about the *welfare* of our fellow human beings, and we must act *honorably* in their midst.

"The Time of God's Patience"

I do quite a bit of reading in the history of democratic thought. While the origins of democratic theory and practice lie in ancient Greece and Rome, much of the significant thought on the subject occurred in the past four centuries or so in Great Britain and the United States. Political thinkers past and present disagree much on many of the issues, but there is some consensus on at least two key points. One is that democratic politics requires a willingness to work at compromises. The other is that democracy at its best is practiced by leaders who are willing to engage each other in intelligent and reasoned debate about the fundamental issues at stake in a civil society.

The Mennonites have a wonderful phrase to describe our present situation as Christians. We are "living in the time of God's patience." If God is patient, we must be also. We need to patiently engage the issues in our democratic system, with a willingness to find less-than-perfect solutions. But it does take some effort to cultivate that kind of patience. It is understandable that if we get genuinely involved in "seeking the welfare" of the larger society in which we live, we will want to succeed in our efforts to bring about some good.

Kuyper offers us an excellent theological basis for working to cultivate that kind of patience. All the square inches of our creation belong to Jesus. God in Christ presently rules over all things and over all people. To be sure, many people in the world today do not acknowledge that fact. They do not recognize the authority of Jesus Christ. Indeed, it isn't just that they refuse to acknowledge his authority — they live in ways that openly oppose God's will.

But someday all of this will be straightened out. Jesus will appear on the clouds "and every eye will see him" (Revelation 1:7). The question for Christians today, then, is the one the young evangelical professionals in Washington were posing: How do we act in the meantime? What is our present responsibility as citizens in societies where people do not acknowledge that there is a God who rules over all things?

The Challenge of Pluralism

For Kuyper, a democratic system provided the best framework for Christian involvement in public life under sinful conditions. He could even wax eloquent, as he did in his Stone Lectures, about how Calvinism has been a major force in history in undergirding democracy. He may have been overstating the historical case a little, but Kuyper was right to insist that, properly understood, there is an intimate link between a belief in God's sovereignty and democratic ideals. If God's authority alone is absolute, then no human government has the right to claim absolute authority over its citizens. And given the propensity toward sinfulness in all human individuals and institutions, governments are not only necessary safeguards against sin, they are themselves affected by our common depravity. Thus the need to both respect government's proper "ordering" role and be clear about its God-ordained limitations.

Kuyper gave much thought to how a society ought to be structured when it encompasses a diversity of belief systems and lifestyles. He was adamant in his refusal to resort to imposing an "established religion" on this diversity. James Bratt puts it nicely: "Kuyper did not want a naked public square but a crowded one," with no belief system "having an official ad-

vantage." Kuyper was endorsing "pluralism under secularization but not secularism" — that is, he was showing us how to
encourage the interaction among a plurality of viewpoints in
a highly secularized culture, but without turning the secular
into an "ism," an ideology that simply leaves God out of the
picture.[1]

On Kuyper's view, the state should act more like a referee
than like a coach or a cheerleader, showing impartiality toward a variety of religious and moral perspectives — as well as
irreligious and immoral ones — while allowing them to com-
pete for the allegiances of citizens within a framework characterized by fair play.

To be sure, support for this kind of "referee" political system does not come easily for those who nurture deep convictions about what is right or wrong. This is why we have to keep
reminding ourselves that there is a Judgment Day coming, but
that it has not yet arrived. We live in a time when righteousness
and unrighteousness exist side by side, and believers must establish their patterns of living with this fact in mind.

It also important to keep reminding ourselves that the
struggle against sin is waged within each human soul. The
line between good and evil cannot be easily drawn between
groups of people. The real conflict is between differing sets of
basic life-guiding principles. Believers may have the right
principles, but they continue to be plagued by their innate
sinfulness. The antithesis reaches into each of us. And because of the workings of common grace, unbelievers often
perform better than we might expect, even when they serve
perverse principles.

1. James D. Bratt, "Introduction: Abraham Kuyper: His World and His
Work," in Bratt, *Abraham Kuyper: A Centennial Reader,* 14-15.

Beyond "Christendom"

———— ∞∞∞ ————

A theologian whom I greatly respect once told me that he was puzzled by my admiration for Kuyper — and especially by my insistence that Kuyper's views are helpful today. "After all," he said, "we are in a post-Christendom period in human history, and Kuyper's thought is still very Constantinian!" No contemporary call for for a Kuyper-type approach to culture in general, and politics in particular, can avoid addressing that issue.

The "post-Christendom" label is a case in point for the considerable talk these days about our being "post" this or that pattern of the past. Earlier I discussed briefly the way in which Kuyper's thought fits nicely in certain respects with the way contemporary "postmodern" thinkers discuss the defects of "the Enlightenment project." Enlightenment thought saw human reason — or more generally, an enlightened human consciousness — as the highest standard in the universe for deciding issues of truth and goodness. On that view, if there is anything worthwhile in religion, we find it by seeing whether it conforms to or even reinforces what we "enlightened" human beings can come to know without the aid of any sort of revelation.

Most of the postmodern thinkers who are asking us to move to a "post-Enlightenment" way of viewing reality are not, as we saw earlier, calling for a return to relying on God as the source of meaning and truth. And even in the Christian world, the demand for a "post-Enlightenment" perspective is not regularly linked to a commitment to classic orthodoxy. But that is precisely what Kuyper was after. He rejected the supremacy of enlightened human consciousness in order to highlight the fact that it is God's will alone that reigns supreme in the universe.

Connecting the "Posts"

Kuyper's rejection of Enlightenment thinking has a close connection to his views about the political arrangement that people have in mind today when they condemn "Christendom." James Bratt points us to the connection when he says that the rejection of the Enlightenment

> enabled the Neo-Calvinists to declare, to their everlasting credit, that reason was the servant of the heart; that no intellectual activity, including the natural sciences, was impartial or value-free or without presuppositions; and that every social organization operated according to and in the interests of an ideology.[1]

Both the Enlightenment and Christendom were linked to ideologies about social organization that Kuyper rejected. In

1. James D. Bratt, *Dutch Calvinism in Modern America: A History of a Conservative Subculture* (Grand Rapids: Eerdmans, 1984), 18.

the case of the Enlightenment, Kuyper saw its philosophical perspective as the inspiration for the French Revolution, in which crowds of people, inspired by the Enlightenment's proclamation of the sovereignty of Reason, set out to overthrow ancient orders and practices, beheading public officials and desecrating places of worship. All of that was a manifestation of a basic project which, as Kuyper put it, "substituted the will of the *individual* for the will of the *Creator of nations.*"[2] When he chose to name his political party "the Anti-Revolutionary Party," it was precisely the French Revolution that he had in mind.

But in opposing the ideology undergirding the French Revolution, Kuyper was not attempting to preserve all that the French Revolution had been bent on destroying. His complaint about the French Revolution was that its ideology was so all-embracing that it used "enlightened" political power to diminish the life of the other spheres. And he had the same kind of worry about the older Constantinian alliance between church and state. Bratt observes that one of Kuyper's key objections to the ideology of the French Revolution was that "it shattered social bonds by valorizing the individual and the ethic of self-interest."[3] In its own way, Constantinianism fostered a similar kind of "shattering," by attempting to subsume all the spheres of life under the control of a church-state alliance.

I should explain here that these days the labels "Constantinianism" and "Christendom" are often used interchangeably. Shortly after the Emperor Constantine converted to

2. Kuyper, *Christianity and the Class Struggle,* 22, n. 5.
3. Bratt, "Introduction," in Bratt, *Abraham Kuyper: A Centennial Reader,* 13.

Christianity early in the fourth century A.D., he issued the Edict of Milan (in 313), not only legalizing Christianity but actually making it the official religion of the Roman Empire. This resulted in such a close relationship between church and state — the "Christendom" arrangement — that infant baptism was for all practical purposes the entry-point into citizenship. Thus, often these days when some religion is seen as being too closely linked to political power, the specter of "Constantinianism" or "Christendom" is quickly raised.

The criticisms of the Constantinian arrangement are legitimate. When the church allies itself too closely with political power it loses the freedom to be the kind of church that God wants it to be. The late Lesslie Newbigin, who served for many years during the twentieth century as a missionary in India, made this case very effectively.[4] When Newbigin returned to the British Isles after his retirement, he was shocked by the major cultural changes that had taken place there as well as on the European continent and in North America. When he began his career he saw himself as being sent out from a Christian culture — where Christianity was "the established religion" — to a mission field. But now he realized that his own homeland had become a mission field. Christians in the West, Newbigin observed, could no longer take a dominant Christian influence for granted. We are now, he said, "post-Christendom." But that is not a thing to be regretted, he quickly added; the church should always see itself as "missional." The Christendom arrangement lured the church into a sense of "owning" the culture that kept it from full faithfulness to the gospel.

4. Lesslie Newbigin, *The Gospel in a Pluralist Society* (Grand Rapids: Eerdmans, 1989).

The Anabaptist Option

All of that can be enthusiastically endorsed by Kuyperians. One of the reasons why Kuyper thought of himself as a "neo-Calvinist" was because he wanted to distance himself from the way that earlier generations of Calvinists had used political power to further the church's cause.

The problem, though, is that sometimes those who make much of the dangers of Constantinianism and Christendom place overly strict limits on how Christians can relate to public life. This was made clear to me in the conversation with the theologian who thought that my affinity with Kuyper meant that I am dangerously close to Constantinianism. I pushed the person to explain why he interpreted my perspective in that manner. His response came in the form of two questions: Do I think that Christians can work effectively for Christian goals "within the American political system"? And do I believe that Christians can not only endorse the use of violence in law enforcement and military campaigns, but actually themselves serve as police and members of the military?

I responded to both questions in the affirmative, but also with the necessary qualifications. I believe that there are limits to the kinds of political compromises that Christians can agree to. And I also believe that police action and military campaigns must be conducted within the kind of moral framework associated with "just war doctrine." The person's response was an "Aha! So you admit it. You really *are* a Constantinian!"

The fact is that my argument with that person has to do with issues that go back at least as far as the Protestant Reformation of the sixteenth century. The Anabaptist wing of the Reformation insisted that the other Protestant movements,

Lutheranism and Calvinism, had not adequately broken with Catholic thought and practice on some crucial issues. "Anabaptism" means "re-baptism," which signifies the Anabaptist rejection of infant baptism. Any person who had been baptized as a baby had to be re-baptized as an adult if that person wanted to join the Anabaptist community. Obviously, this insistence was in good part based on questions of biblical interpretation. But the Anabaptists also argued that, because of the Constantinian arrangement, infant baptism was too closely tied to the idea of citizenship. They called for the church to be a community of disciples — of persons who make a conscious adult decision, signified in baptism by immersion, to follow the Way of the Cross — who live with a clear sense of being over-against the dominant culture. This over-against-ness includes both a commitment to nonviolence and a refusal to serve as agents of the worldly "powers that be."

The debate about such matters is still alive, with many influential Christian leaders today arguing that the gospel calls us to a way of life so antithetical to the patterns of collective life in the larger human culture that Christians are required, in effect, to create an alternative culture. One influential example of such thinking is a book co-authored by Stanley Hauerwas and William Willimon, *Resident Aliens,* in which the authors issue an Anabaptist-type call for the formation of a Kingdom community living in separation from the practices of the larger human community, especially those practices that are closely aligned with the political assumptions of secular thought.[5]

5. Stanley Hauerwas and William Willimon, *Resident Aliens: Life in the Christian Colony* (Nashville: Abingdon Press, 1989).

Responsible Power

I take an important clue on this subject from Lesslie Newbigin. As critical as he was of the Constantinian/Christendom arrangement, he insisted that we must be careful in our assessment of what the errors of that arrangement were. "Much has been written," he observed, "about the harm done to the cause of the gospel when Constantine accepted baptism, and it is not difficult to expatiate on this theme." There can be no question, Newbigin said, that the church has regularly fallen "into the temptation of worldly power." But he goes on: Should we conclude from this that the proper alternative was for the church simply to "have . . . washed its hands of responsibility for the political order"? Do we really think, Newbigin asks, that the cause of the gospel would have been better served "if the church had refused all political responsibility, if there had never been a 'Christian' Europe"? The fact is, he notes, that the Constantinian project had its origins in a creative response to a significant cultural challenge. There was in Constantine's day, he says, a spiritual crisis in the larger culture, and people "turned to the church as the one society that could hold a disintegrating world together." And for all the mistakes that were made along the way, it was nonetheless a good thing that the church actively took up this challenge.[6]

This is an insightful analysis, and there is every reason to think that Kuyper would agree with Newbigin. For Kuyper, there is nothing wrong with working within the present politi-

6. Lesslie Newbigin, *Foolishness to the Greeks: The Gospel and Western Culture* (Grand Rapids: Eerdmans, 1986), 100-101.

cal structures to serve the cause of righteousness in the world. But we must always do so with an awareness of the Constantinian danger of forming an unhealthy — and unfaithful — alliance between the church and political power.

When Spheres "Shrink"

———— ∞∞∞ ————

I want to return to my earlier example of the mother and son: she was his dean, his elder, and his mother — three different spheres, with three different authority patterns. The ecclesial bond is different from the familial bond. Churches are churches; they are not families. Each mode of association has its own place in the divine ordering of human life.

I accept that Kuyperian way of viewing the spheres. But I have also thought much in recent years about what happens when one or more spheres begin to weaken. What happens then? Is it possible for one sphere to take over the functions of another sphere?

Civility and Meals

Some of my re-thinking — or at least re-casting — Kuyper's thought on this subject has been stimulated by my work on the topic of civility. When I first began writing a book on that subject,[1] I became convinced of the importance of the family meal as a kind of training ground for civility. I get this in part from the ancient philosopher Aristotle. He said that when we become citizens we have to go beyond our kinship bonds. We have to respect other citizens not because they are our own flesh and blood — which most of them are not — but simply because they are human.

It is important to emphasize, though, that Aristotle was saying that in public life, as adult citizens, we have to go *beyond* kinship bonds. Only after we have been "schooled" in kinship relationships are we ready to go to the next step of citizenship. Learning to relate to other people as citizens presupposes what we have learned in families. In order for babies to grow up into good citizens they need first to experience maturation as members of families.

Citizenship is in trouble today. As I write this, there is a lot of commentary in the popular media about the rise of incivility. People don't seem to know how to respect each other. They shout at those with whom they disagree without actually listening to them.

One cause of all of this, as I see things, is the decline of the family meal. At a presentation I once attended, sponsored by people who provide food services for college campuses, a person said that young people today don't know how to "dine"; instead they "graze." They don't sit at a table with other people for any length of time. In a college eating area, they go from the salad bar to the hot meal counter, and then pick up a frozen yogurt cone as they leave. And this pattern of eating be-

---

1. Richard J. Mouw, *Uncommon Decency: Christian Civility in an Uncivil World* (Downers Grove: InterVarsity Press, 1992; revised and expanded edition, 2010).

gins in their homes. If family members eat together at all, it is often with the TV set on.

In the old-style family meal, children learned manners. They cultivated patience — by being forced to sit at a table for forty minutes with people they found irritating. This prepared them for citizenship.

The decline of the family meal is itself a symptom of a decline in family life as such. For one thing, few of us have the same access to an extended family that people once did. We move around frequently, and more of us come from broken families. Hectic schedules and scattered lives keep us from some of the important benefits of family time.

Compensating for Sphere-Weakness

Again, I still think Kuyper was right about the spheres. Families are different than churches; businesses are different than universities; and so on. Each occupies an important place in the array of God-ordained spheres of interaction.

The problem, of course, is that in many situations one of those spheres becomes severely weakened. That is what I see happening these days in families: a case of "sphere shrinkage." This is a real loss. It is not the way God intended it to be. And until we can rebuild the family, we have to engage in what we might think of as "sphere compensation." This means taking careful account of what we have lost in a case of sphere shrinkage, and then compensating for that — at least on a temporary basis — by building the lost or weakened functions into some other sphere, so that another sphere can compensate for the loss by taking on additional cultural "work."

I believe it is important for the church today to provide some infrastructural support for dealing with the problem of sphere shrinkage in family life. By seeing this as a compensatory strategy — the church should work to restore the family's independence — we can still affirm Kuyper's insistence that we be clear about the differences between family and church in the divine design.

A Church "Family"

Fuller Theological Seminary has a creative and flourishing program — the Fuller Youth Institute[2] — that focuses on the study of young people, bringing together research from psychologists with expertise in youth ministry and cross-cultural relations. One key area of our research is in what is called "asset theory" in understanding adolescent development. Instead of concentrating on what makes kids go bad — access to weapons, alcohol, and drugs, exposure to family violence, and the like — we study what makes good kids turn out well. Among other resources, we draw on the work done at the Search Institute in Minneapolis, where researchers have developed a list of what they label "40 Developmental Assets for adolescents (ages 12-18)."[3]

The whole list is interesting, but for my purposes here, the first three Developmental Assets are especially significant. The first factor that promotes adolescent psychological health is "Family Support," specifically love and nurture. The

---

2. http://fulleryouthinstitute.org/.

3. http://www.search-institute.org/content/40-developmental-assets-adolescents-ages-12-18.

second is "Positive Family Communication" — not only do the researchers recommend a lot of actual talking between parents and children, but they also insist on frequent mutual communication between younger and older in the immediate family as well as with distant relatives, by emails, notes, and cards.

The third Developmental Asset, though, moves beyond the kinship system to "Other Adult Relationships." The Search Institute recommends that a young person should receive very frequent caring support from three or more persons to whom he or she is not closely related. This obviously can come from coaches, teachers, counselors, scouting leaders, and the like. But it seems obvious to us that a congregation should play a significant role in this regard.

Unfortunately, the approach of many of our churches is actually counterproductive in this area. They segregate youth — in worship and the arrangement of meeting spaces — in a way that deliberately separates the generations. This needs to be reversed. But it is especially important that one-to-one relationships be formed. An adult who is not related to a specific teenager can greet the young person at church — making eye contact — and ask what the adult can pray for in that teenager's life during the next week. And then a follow-up a week later: How did that test go? Did you win the game? Anything new in that relationship?

That's fairly practical stuff. Small groups, intergenerational in composition, can also accomplish much. And, of course, dining together — no grazing!

The Challenge of Islam

———— ∞∞∞ ————

Kuyper frequently gave talks to women's groups. Fifty of these talks are collected in a little volume, *Women of the Old Testament.* To refer to many of the women whom Kuyper discusses would draw blank stares from most Christians these days. But Kuyper obviously paid close attention to the likes of Rizpah and the mother of Ichabod and "the peasant woman of Bahurim." However obscure or marginal these women may seem to a story, he insisted, they are there because they have some significance in God's overall plan.

Kuyper is especially interested in Hagar in this regard. She is there in the biblical account, he says, "for a more significant reason than merely to excite our sympathy for her at losing her way with her son in the desert." She serves an important role "as a link in the chain of God's unfathomable Providence."[1] One reason for her importance, Kuyper points out, is that the Apostle Paul refers to her in Galatians 4:22-27,

1. Abraham Kuyper, *Women of the Old Testament,* trans. Henry Zylstra (Grand Rapids: Zondervan Publishing House, 1934), 19.

where Sarah and Hagar are seen as symbols of two different relationships to God. The spiritual offspring of Sarah are those who have accepted Christ, while Hagar's spiritual descendents remain in their sinful state.

But that is not the whole story about Hagar's significance, says Kuyper. The Lord gives her some "rich promises," especially the one that says that the descendents of Ishmael — the Arab peoples — would have great influence on the earth. And "[h]ow significantly striking it is," says Kuyper, "that in the coming of the Mohammedans this entire prophecy has been literally fulfilled."[2]

Assessing Islam

While Kuyper did not have a detailed knowledge of a variety of non-Christian religions, it is obvious that he had a special fascination with Islam. Early on in his Stone Lectures, for example, he sets forth a contrast between "Paganism" and "Islamism." The Pagan perspective, he observes, denies God's transcendence; it tries to contain God within what we Christians know to be the created order, resulting in an outlook that "surmises, assumes and worships God in the creature." Muslim thought, in contrast, operates with a clear sense of the great being-gap between Creator and creation: it "isolates God from the creature, in order to avoid all commingling with the creature." Thus it stands as an "absolute antithesis to Paganism."[3]

In its antithetical relationship to Pagan thought, the Mus-

2. Kuyper, *Women*, 19.
3. Kuyper, *Lectures*, 20.

lim religion plays an important historical role. In his Hagar meditation, Kuyper notes that Muslims "in large territories have served to set up a protecting wall against heathendom," having "vanquished heathen strength" in places like Africa and Asia. In this regard, Islam serves as a judgment on Christianity, confronting Pagan culture in a way that the church has often failed to do.[4]

Needless to say, Kuyper does not see Islam as embodying a consistent system of revealed truth. He is blunt in giving his assessment of Islam as a "false faith," in that it commits the "fatal error" of refusing to accept Jesus as the promised Messiah, instead placing "a false prophet above him."[5] Without the Savior who has drawn near to us, taking our sins upon himself at Calvary, Islam is left with "no second birth, no deep concern about sin, no soteriological content."[6]

But having issued that sternly negative verdict, Kuyper also observes that the Muslim religion "remains enveloped in mist." The fact is that through Islam, millions "have come to believe in one God, and in God's prophetical revelation." And Muslims do honor Jesus as one of the prophets. This means, though, that "they remain stranded in the Old Testament and reject the fulfillment of the New. In its stead they place that other fulfillment which is contained in the Koran."[7]

Kuyper clearly shows some ambivalence about Islam. He is positive about the way that Muslims see the will of Allah as

4. Kuyper, *Women*, 18-19.
5. Kuyper, *Women*, 18.
6. Rimmer De Vries, "Kuyper on Islam: a Summary and Translation" (a summary in English of an essay Kuyper wrote in 1905 on "The Enigma of Islam"), in Gordon Graham, ed., *The Kuyper Center Review* (Grand Rapids: Eerdmans, 2010), 140.
7. Kuyper, *Women*, 18-19.

speaking to the whole of created life. In making this point, he describes the Muslim perspective in very "Kuyperian" terms: "Muhammed's religion," he observes, "was not something confined to the upper room, outside the daily life of the believer, but affected all of life, penetrated all human existence and activity, society, government, etc. Allah's power embraced everything, and besides Allah nothing could be tolerated."[8]

Help for the Present

Many of my fellow evangelicals these days have a difficult time with the very idea of Muslim-Christian dialogue. To be sure, evangelicals often have problems with the notion of dialogue as such. We have not always found it easy to engage in calm give-and-take with those whom we disagree with on fundamental issues.

But Islam presents a special challenge. For one thing, both evangelicalism and Islam are fairly aggressive at seeking converts. Each community has a clear sense of what it takes for an individual to become right with God. And given what we each believe, we can't both be right.

Nor does it help that in some places in the world, Christians experience persecution at the hands of Muslims. There are even contexts where Islamic governments have made it a capital offense for a Muslim to become a Christian.

And then there is the fact that the Koran honors Jesus as a prophet, but denies that he died on the cross. With other religious groups, Christians have faced serious disagreement

8. De Vries, "Kuyper on Islam," 139.

about the *significance* of what happened on Calvary. But with Muslims, we can't even agree that the crucifixion *happened!*

None of this makes for an encouraging climate for dialogue. But the fact is, we have much to talk about. And Kuyper's comments about Islam point the way to at least one important topic for conversation: our different ways of experiencing and understanding the divine call to serve the cause of righteousness in all areas of life.

A Kinship of Sorts

While thinking about a Kuyper-inspired approach to Islam, I came across a magazine column criticizing the way President Obama has discussed Islam in some of his speeches. The columnist, Leon Wieseltier, referred to "Obama's creepy habit of addressing Muslims in religious terms." What Mr. Obama's rhetoric fails to recognize, said Wieseltier, is that the main conflict relating to Islam these days is not one between the Muslim religion and the rest of society. Rather it is the battle *within* Islam, between those who focus exclusively on religious categories and those who are working toward the "secularization" of Muslim life.[9] And Wieseltier was not subtle in telling us which segment of contemporary Islam he finds "creepy."

The truth is that Mr. Wieseltier would also find Kuyper, and those of us who agree with Kuyper's approach to issues of public life, to be creepy. Like Muslims of deep conviction, we oppose much that is associated with the idea of "secularization" in the mind of someone like Leon Wieseltier.

9. Leon Wieseltier, "Showdown," *The New Republic,* April 29, 2010, 48.

That some of us in the Christian world see some common ground with Islam on these matters is recognized by Ian Buruma in his insightful little book *Taming the Gods: Religion and Democracy on Three Continents*. In discussing the hostility that many in Europe express regarding the growth of Muslim communities in their midst, Buruma sees that opposition as having much to do with the way in which the Muslim presence is viewed as a significant force for resisting the secularization of life in the West. And then he makes special mention of evangelicalism: the evangelical movement in North America, he says, has much in common on this score with Muslims in Europe.[10]

Deep Convictions in a Pluralistic World

This is the kind of commonality that Kuyper recognized. The shared profession of belief in the God of Abraham establishes some sort of common ground. Christians and Muslims have somewhat similar understandings of the nature of the human person and of the present human condition. We each believe, for example, that we human beings, if left on our own, cannot find the path to eternal blessedness. We both insist that we need a revelation from God, a God who in turn must redirect our wills toward himself, providing us with those commandments — those prescriptions for righteousness that we could never come up with on our own — that show us the way in which we must walk if we are to be directed toward our eternal destinies.

10. Ian Buruma, *Taming the Gods: Religion and Democracy on Three Continents* (Princeton: Princeton University Press, 2010), 7.

There is another factor, however, that is especially important for our focus here on our respective roles in public life. Our religious beliefs are for each of our communities matters of *deep conviction*. And each of our communities worries much about the ways in which many of the dominant patterns of the larger culture — especially the larger culture of the West — pose a serious threat to the maintenance of these deep convictions.

The huge challenge that we face in this regard is: how do we live out our faith in a pluralistic society in which we acknowledge the rights of our fellow citizens — people whose values, beliefs, and lifestyles we often strongly disagree with — to enjoy the same freedoms that we claim for ourselves? This is a topic about which Muslims and evangelicals have much to discuss together. We both operate with equally strong convictions that we bring with us into the public arena — those deeply held beliefs that in good part go against the grain of the dominant cultures of the West.

The Reason for Our Hope

It is precisely here, though, that Muslims and Christians need to talk honestly with each other. As I discussed earlier, evangelicals have often acted as if there are only two options in understanding our role in public life. Either we think we have to withdraw from any active concern for public life, consigning ourselves to surviving spiritually on the margins of culture, or we decide to call on our Christian troops to try to take it over, attempting to enforce "Christian" laws and practices.

It should be clear from what I have been spelling out in these pages that Kuyper thinks that these options — withdraw or take over — constitute a false choice. There is a way for Christians to work actively to bring the concerns of our faith to the larger culture, a way that recognizes that we cannot have it all during this "time of God's patience." It is not only an interesting possibility to talk with Muslims about how we understand our public callings in our pluralistic world — it is an urgent matter.

To be sure, we have many other things to discuss with Muslims. Most important, we need to share our testimonies about what each of us sees as the kind of spiritual resources that we can draw upon for cultivating the patience and strength that can sustain us in the here-and-now. This is an important agenda item for us as Christians who have been commanded to "always be ready to make your defense to anyone who demands from you an account of the hope that is in you" (1 Peter 3:15). And this means, for Christians, that we will look for opportunities to talk about the Risen Lord who has guaranteed the ultimate victory over all that threatens the *shalom* — the *salaam* — that God intends for the whole creation.

Again, we can hope to find the opportunities to talk about those supremely important matters with our Muslim friends. But Kuyper points us to some common concerns that can serve to get the conversation started.

A Kuyperianism "Under the Cross"

———— ∞∞∞ ————

W hen I wrote my book on Christian civility, I entitled one of my chapters "Abraham Kuyper, Meet Mother Teresa."[1] I paid my dues to Kuyper — gladly so — by testifying to my fondness for his bold affirmation that Christ calls out "Mine!" about every square inch of the created order. It all belongs to him. That is a wonderful proclamation. But I also expressed a worry about how that "Mine!" manifesto has sometimes been used — not only by folks who have learned it from Kuyper, but also by Kuyper himself on occasion.

Looking to Calvary

The evangelical historian Mark Noll once said of Kuyper's "not one square inch" proclamation that "no truer words could ever be spoken," for it gives us a

1. Chapter 12 of my 1992 edition of *Uncommon Decency;* Chapter 13 in the 2010 edition.

dramatic picture of Christ, transfigured in glory, hand outstretched, finger extended in commanding power, standing over the halls of Congress, the White House, the United Nations, the state legislature, the local school board, the tax assessor's office, and the weary citizen sitting at home reading the front page of the local newspaper, and declaring with full yet winsome authority, "This too is mine!"

All that is truly inspiring, says Noll. "Yet it may be," he goes on to observe, "that this picture is not quite complete." The Jesus who points us to all that territory that he claims as his own is a Savior whose "footprints are spattered blood. And the hand that points is marked with a wound." To follow this Jesus, says Noll, is to remember "the road to Calvary that the Lord Jesus took to win his place of command."[2]

Noll's point has to be taken seriously by those who are seeking to apply Kuyper's insights to present-day cultural realties. Kuyper's manifesto about Jesus crying out "Mine!" is a call to arms, a rallying of the troops to go out into those square inches — politics, the entertainment industry, corporate life, journalism — to battle the foe and reclaim territory for Jesus. But a "culture wars" mentality has been all too prevalent in recent years, and we do not need to reinforce it with a selective use of Kuyper's thought. The example of Mother Teresa, giving loving comfort to dying lepers on the streets of Calcutta, is a necessary corrective to the triumphalist spirit.

2. Mark A. Noll, with responses by James D. Bratt, Max L. Stackhouse, and James W. Skillen, *Adding Cross to Crown: The Political Significance of Christ's Passion* (Grand Rapids: Baker Books and the Center for Public Justice, 1996), 46.

"Mine!" Proclaimed in Love

I once saw a brief news clip of a party held after an annual Academy Awards ceremony. An Oscar winner, in a rush of enthusiasm (probably fueled by alcohol), held the statuette aloft and screamed, "I won it! It's mine!"

That's not the sense of the "Mine!" that Jesus proclaims about the whole creation. His use of "Mine!" is more like that of a mother who lovingly whispers "You're my own little baby" to the infant in her arms, or the husband who says as he embraces his wife, "You will always be mine."

There's a nice story told about Pope John XIII, when he was still Venice's Cardinal Roncalli. He was having dinner one night with a priestly assistant who was reporting to the cardinal about another priest, a bit of a renegade, who was doing things that were embarrassing the hierarchy. The future pope listened calmly, sipping wine from a goblet. Finally the assistant cried out in a frustrated tone, "How can you take this so calmly? Don't you realize what this priest is doing?" The cardinal then gently asked the younger priest, "Father, whose goblet is this?" "It is yours, Your Eminence," the priest answered. The cardinal then threw the goblet to the floor, and it shattered into many fragments. "And now whose goblet is it?" he asked. "It is still yours," was the answer. "And so is this priest still my brother in Christ," said the cardinal with a note of sadness in his voice, "even though he is shattered and broken."

Jesus often says "Mine!" with that kind of gentle sadness — and people like me all too often provoke such gentle sadness from him. He longs for the day — a day that is surely coming — when he will say a joyful "Mine!" over the creation that he has made new. That "Mine!" will finally have no sadness to it.

Until that day comes, however, we have no business shouting Jesus' "Mine!" with any kind of arrogance. I worry about that tendency toward arrogance. It can easily blind us to the need to go out and suffer in those many broken regions of creation where the homeless set up their crude sleeping shelters, where people grieve, and where the abused and the abandoned cry out in despair. Jesus calls us to join him there, for those square inches — and those who inhabit them — belong to him, too.

Mother Teresa grasped that sense of Christ's concern for the suffering. She would tell her sister-nuns that they had to study the New Testament very carefully, so that they would recognize Jesus "in his dreadful disguise among the poorest of the poor" out on the streets of Calcutta.

Again: Abraham Kuyper, meet Mother Teresa.

"Under the Cross"

To be sure, we can be inspired to reclaim the creation for Christ by Kuyper's bold proclamation that the ascended Christ presently rules over all things. But to serve that reign in this present world is to recognize that the triumphant Christ is still a grieving Savior, coming to bring healing to the wounded creation that he came to save.

One of Kuyper's Dutch biographers, George Puchinger, once told an audience the story of Kuyper's last hours. As the great man lay dying, no longer capable of speech, with his loved ones gathered around him, he lifted his eyes to the crucifix that hung on the wall above his bed, and pointed to the image of the Savior on the cross.

I like to think that in that silent gesture Kuyper was leaving us with an important message. It is a message embodying a theme with which he was very familiar. His Dutch Calvinist community had known much suffering in its past, and he knew that history well. When that community experienced times of persecution, even martyrdom, for their faith, they had a way of explaining their condition: they called themselves "churches under the cross." That is a good image for our own service today: Christians must care deeply about culture, and they must recognize that true cultural obedience to their Lord has to take place under the cross.

ANDY CROUCH